Writing Journals

Grades 4–6

Activities Across the Curriculum

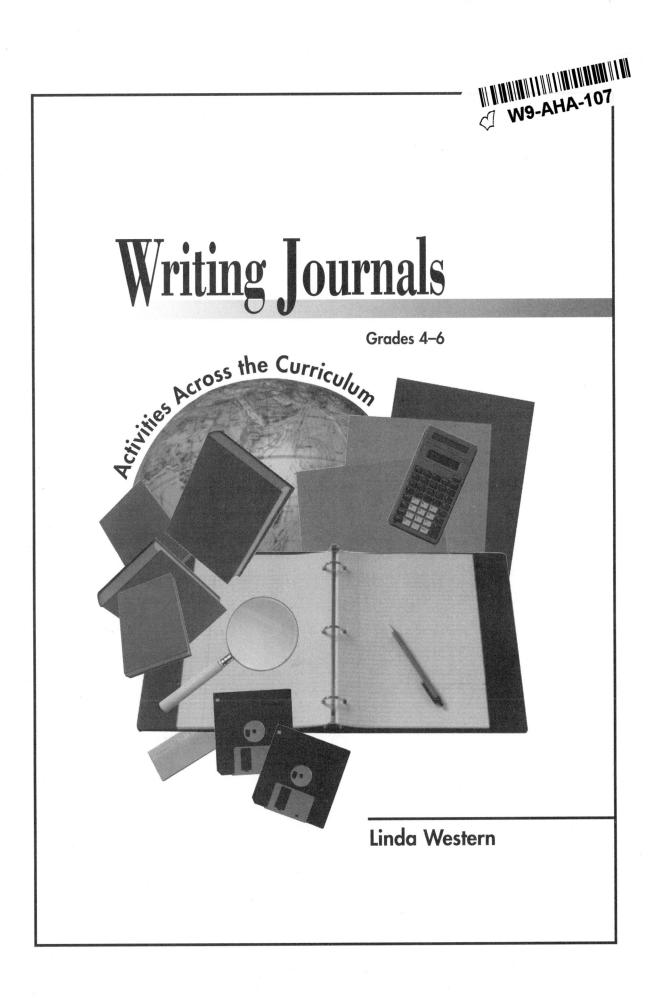

Linda Western

To Sarah, John and Rich, who continue to make remarkable tracks of their own.

Special thanks go to Sydney Janicek and Amanda Hollister, students at Saukville Elementary School, for contributing their journal entries to this book.

GoodYearBooks

are available for most basic curriculum subjects plus many enrichment areas. For more GoodYearBooks, contact your local bookseller or educational dealer. For a complete catalog with information about other GoodYearBooks, please write:

GoodYearBooks
1900 East Lake Avenue
Glenview, IL 60025

Design by Nancy Rudd

Preface

*E*ach track tells a story. As you follow the marks an animal has left behind, you get to know it: where it goes, what it likes to eat, when it runs, and why. As you begin to see the patterns in the tracks, you will begin to see the variations. Each set of tracks is unique, because each animal's life is different from every other's and each day its path is a little different from the one it took the day before.

Betsy Bowen, Tracks in the Wild
(Boston: Little, Brown and Company, 1993.)

There are parallels between writing and making tracks. Our writings tell a story, too, often revealing us as people whose needs, interests, and wishes are much like those of others. But like the tracks in nature, what we write also highlights our differences—from each other and within ourselves from day to day.

Observers in the wild need good luck or great skill to find the tracks animals leave behind, and some tracks last only until the next change of weather. But our tracks—what we write—can be kept ready at hand, for as long as we want to consult them, or we can change them at whim. Eventually, if we write often and thoughtfully enough, some of the tracks we leave will prove to be useful, enlightening, amusing, maybe even astonishing.

This book is all about leaving tracks, lots of them, where we can always find them: in logs, journals, and notebooks.

Contents

A Gathering of Ideas 1

How Is *Writing Journals* Organized? 1

An Emphasis on Collaboration and Cooperation....................... 2

What's So Special About Journals?... 3

The Link Between Writing and Learning................................... 3

How Can *Writing Journals* Help? 4

Some Journal Basics.. 7

Journals Come in Many Varieties... 7

What Makes a Good Journal? 8

Is There Enough Time for Journal Writing?.............................. 8

What About Grades? 9

What About Punctuation and Spelling?................................... 10

What About Privacy? 10

What About Journals and the Bilingual Student?..................... 11

What About Computers? 11

A Few More Words About Dialogue Journals............................ 11

Getting Started 13

The Teacher as a Model... 13

Launching a New Area of Study 13

Beginning with Personal Experiences....................................... 14

Pointing to Others Who Have Kept Journals 15

Helping Children to See Why Journal Writing Is Important 15

Journal Writing and Literature... 17

Overview 18

Learning Logs... 19

Reader Response Journals 30

Writers' Notebooks 42

Children's Books Referred to in This Section 49

Sources on Book Making 49

Journal Writing and Social Studies 51

    Overview 52

    Learning Logs 53

    Reader Response Journals 62

    Writers' Notebooks 72

    A Sampling of Trickster Tales 78

    A Sampling of Folk Tale Variants 79

    A Sampling of Myths Exploring the Seasons 80

    Other Children's Books Referred to in This Section 80

Journal Writing and Science 81

    Overview 82

    Learning Logs 83

    Reader Response Journals 95

    Writers' Notebooks 104

    Children's Books Referred to in This Section 111

Journal Writing and Mathematics 113

    Overview 114

    Learning Logs 115

    Reader Response Journals 124

    Writers' Notebooks 130

    Children's Books Referred to in This Section 133

Where to Learn More 135

    References 135

    A Selection of Software Programs 138

From *Writing Journals*, published by GoodYearBooks. Copyright © 1996 Linda Western.

A Gathering of Ideas

Currently, information about journals and discussions of journal-writing activities are scattered throughout curriculum guides, textbooks, and articles; they also are shared by teachers in anecdotes and other professional exchanges. In order to make teachers' work with journals a little easier, *Writing Journals* brings many of these ideas together into one place.

The suggestions you will read about here have developed out of classroom practice. And, because experience shows that journal writing has a place throughout the curriculum, these suggestions pertain to study in literature, social studies, science, and mathematics, with several ideas involving music and art added for good measure. (You will often find that the suggested study is interdisciplinary.) Each activity is paired with an extension that carries the initial inquiry forward in some way.

Many different experiences and resources serve as catalysts for these journal activities. Some are based on children's day-to-day life at home, in school, and in the community; others involve experiments, surveys, and research. Some activities draw on children's own thoughts, ideas, and memories. Others focus on what children can learn from external resources: from conversations with people they already know and people they meet, from newspapers, television, radio and movies, from books and magazines, from nature, and from the languages of mathematics and science.

How Is *Writing Journals* Organized?

Journals come in many varieties, each calling for a somewhat different sort of engagement by children. No one type is necessarily better than another, but some apply more readily than others in the curricular areas of the middle grades.

In *Writing Journals,* we focus on four types: dialogue journals, learning logs, reader response journals, and writers' notebooks (see pages 7–8 for a description of each). Dialogue journals are discussed for all subject areas on pages 11–12. Ideas for journal writing in the other three types are found in each of the subject area sections: literature, social studies, science and mathematics.

For each subject area, the suggestions within the **Learning Logs, Reader Response Journals,** and **Writers' Notebooks** sections are categorized under two additional headings: **Observations and Interactions** and **Exploration and Research.** The basis for categorization relates to the scope of the suggested journal-writing activities. Those grouped under **Observations and Interactions** engage children in journal writing that begins with what they already know, or what they can learn easily from experiences in their immediate environments. Those labeled **Exploration and**

	Learning Logs		Reader Response Journals		Writers' Notebooks	
	Observations & Interactions	Exploration & Research	Observations & Interactions	Exploration & Research	Observations & Interactions	Exploration & Research
Literature	✔	✔	✔	✔	✔	✔
Social Studies	✔	✔	✔	✔	✔	✔
Science	✔	✔	✔	✔	✔	✔
Mathematics	✔	✔	✔	✔	✔	✔

Research lead children into journal writing that originates with an examination of what others have said or written, or engage them in experiences where the outcome is unknown—experiments or surveys, for example.

The grouping of ideas within these chapters is intended to help you envision possibilities for journal writing within your classrooms. However, your teaching experiences together with the interests and abilities of your students will be the best guide to your use of these suggestions. For example, you may see that a suggestion in the **Science** section could be adapted for work in a Social Studies unit, or that an activity labeled **Observations and Interactions** really could be thought of as an **Exploration and Research** project. Perhaps some of the ideas will prompt you to devise your own variations or invent entirely new activities for involving children in journal writing. *Writing Journals* invites you to tailor its contents to suit your individual classrooms.

An Emphasis on Collaboration and Cooperation

All of the activities presented here engage children in sharing what they have written. In the case of dialogue journals, the conversations are between students and their teachers. In activities involving learning logs, reader response journals, and writers' notebooks, other audiences are involved: classmates, other students in the school, families, people in the broader community.

You also will find that most activities engage children in working together—getting responses from others to initial drafts and then reworking material, pooling individual ideas into a group report or action plan, and so on. Why? When we learn together, our individual thinking is augmented by the thinking of others. We learn to see our work as others see it. Collaborative work also offers valuable practice. After all, that is the way work gets done outside of school.

Now, before taking a closer look at specific activities, let's spend the next few pages exploring answers to the question, "What's so special about journals?"

From *Writing Journals*, published by GoodYearBooks. Copyright © 1996 Linda Western.

What's So Special About Journals?

Chances are that few of us kept journals of the sort described on the following pages when we were in elementary school, and probably not in high school or college, either. Oh, we had spiral notebooks or pocket folders where we dutifully recorded lecture notes, lab experiments, and math proofs. But that's not the sort of writing we will be exploring here.

Our school notebooks and folders—the ones we may still have in cardboard boxes in our attics—served primarily as repositories for the thoughts of other people: our teachers, textbook authors, and most likely the writers of the encyclopedia articles we relied on for writing so many reports. But the student journals, logs, and notebooks we'll be discussing in *Writing Journals* are different.

We will be talking about journal writing that captures the output of children's own inventions. We will see that journals can serve as places where children note what they are observing, imagining, wondering about, and worrying over, until they are ready to take these ideas up again. And we will see that, like tracks in nature, the writing children do in journals can show us where they have been and where they are headed—here as learners in study across the curriculum.

The Link Between Writing and Learning

Learning theorists and educators agree that we learn better and understand more when we associate new information with what we already know. Each of us can recall experiences of our own that verify this idea. But how do we make these connections? One way is by writing—by putting down a record of what we've noticed and by thinking it over on paper. Again, our own experiences provide the proof. All of us know the satisfaction that comes after trying to bring an idea into focus when we are finally able to get it just right by putting it into words.

Journals can be places where children put things into words on a regular basis. And, as children write, their entries can help them to name, describe, explain, and wonder about things in their own lives, enabling them to make connections between what they already know or believe and the new things they want to learn as they grow up. In this way, writing provides its own rewards. As children look through their journals, they will see the "tracks" they have left—evidence of where they have been, what they have done, and how their experience has shaped their thinking.

Writing of this sort also can foster learning in school. We know that students of all ages learn more enthusiastically and efficiently when their schoolwork engages them fully, touching on their own sense of how things are in the world. Study after study shows that youngsters attain greater subject mastery when they are absorbed in work that feels important to them and that they recognize as leading to meaningful results. Writing by children can play a key role in this engagement, just as it does for adults. Nancie Atwell, whose compelling books and lectures emphasize the benefits of involving children in writing, issues a call to action on this point: "I am suggesting that teachers of every discipline might ask students to think and write as scientists, historians, mathematicians and literary critics do—to use writing-as-process to discover meaning just as these scholars do when they go about the real, messy business of thinking on paper" (Atwell, 1990, xiii).

How Can *Writing Journals* Help?

Merely owning a journal doesn't guarantee a thing. Students won't automatically use their journals in ways that help them make connections with what they know and what they are learning. Nor will students, on their own, necessarily make optimal use of writing in their school subject areas. They will benefit from guidance.

That's where this guide comes in. *Writing Journals* provides teachers with a wide variety of ideas for using journal writing effectively across the curriculum in grades four to six. *Writing Journals* gathers together, in one place, many of the best ideas currently under discussion in professional journals and textbooks. It interprets these ideas concretely and extends them to new applications.

Several premises about children and journal writing underlie *Writing Journals*:

1 Unlike private writing in diaries, the journal writing discussed here is meant to be shared. In the case of dialogue journals, the audience is usually one other person—the teacher (see pages 11–12). In the other cases, journal, log, and notebook entries are shared regularly with classmates. Further, these entries often serve as early versions of writing that is later directed to many different audiences:

friends, family, others in the school, and people in more broadly defined communities.

2 Because writing can foster learning in all areas of the curriculum, *Writing Journals* offers suggestions for how to integrate writing with the study of literature, social studies, mathematics, and science. Often the activities lead to interdisciplinary study. With experience, children will soon discover the importance of writing in these subject areas for themselves. How? Ann E. Berthoff provides a succinct explanation: "Those learning to write can learn a great deal from seeing how the scientist's work is related to the poet's and how what the historian does is close to both. As thinkers and formers, interpreters and creators—as composers and writers—they are all naming the world..." (Berthoff, 1987, 17).

3 Journal entries aren't finished products. They represent early states in a child's thinking about an idea. For this reason, journal entries should not be graded. We would not, after all, grade an artist's preliminary sketches. But because journal writing is assumed here to be part of the mathematics, science, social studies and literature programs, the following journal activities lead directly to further study, and some of the final products that emerge from this extended work may be graded according to ordinary classroom grading practices. (See pages 9–10 for a discussion of journals and grading.)

4 Most of the following activities are not intended as one-time events, nor should they be considered as a series of assignments.

From *Writing Journals*, published by GoodYearBooks. Copyright © 1996 Linda Western.

Many should be repeated, in new contexts and/or with different materials. These activities will be particularly valuable when children discover their growing ability to use them as learning tools.

5 Students work harder and are more thoughtful about their writing after they have had instruction—both in content and procedures. (This is a central point throughout Nancie Atwell's *Coming to Know: Writing to Learn in the Intermediate Grades*, and is borne out in the experience of countless educators.) Therefore *Writing Journals* contains a number of suggestions for presentations of subject matter content that can serve as preludes to, and contexts for, journal-writing activities.

6 These activities are designed to provide children with choices—sometimes in topic, sometimes in how they go about studying a topic, and often in how they write about what they are learning. With these choices comes a sense of responsibility for effort and results.

7 As in the case of developing any other valued skill, journal writing requires an investment of time and energy. To record journal entries with ease, children (and teachers) will need practice. They will need to establish the habit of writing as they learn. They also will need to practice ways of getting the most from what they have written—from studying their own tracks!

Some Journal Basics

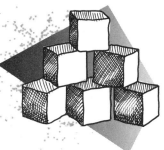

Journals Come in Many Varieties

Children's journals have acquired a number of different names. They are sometimes called day-books, thinkbooks, logs, learning logs, field notebooks, diaries, dialectical notebooks, dialogue journals, literature response journals, writers' notebooks, and writers' journals. Some of these names are essentially synonymous; others refer to specific variations on the journal idea.

Writing Journals focuses on four variations: **dialogue journals, learning logs, reader response journals,** and **writers' notebooks.** All four can be used in the subject areas of grades four to six.

1 DIALOGUE JOURNALS are really conversations in writing. Typically, the two conversation partners are a student and his/her teacher, and their conversations are not shared with others. The teacher plays a central part in a dialogue journal activity. Research and experience show that children write in their journals with more interest and commitment when their teacher writes back (Calkins, 1986). "The teacher's responses… create the motivation and provide the models of thought and reflection of unpredictability and honesty which students need" (Staton, 1987, 56). See pages 11–12 for a further discussion of dialogue journals.

2 LEARNING LOGS typically focus on study in a particular subject area. They provide students with a place to record what they are learning. Less personal than dialogue journals, learning logs help students learn to notice how something is being learned. Content will vary: observations, questions, lists, comparisons, notations of similarities and differences—the learning log possibilities are as varied as our thoughts might be on any given topic. Entries can be made in words or numbers, in graphs or charts, even in pictures.

3 READER RESPONSE JOURNALS provide various means for children to use in reacting to the books they are reading. Again, the entries can be various: questions, comparisons, notations of highlights or complaints, or evaluations; the list of possibilities is a long one. Reader response journals also help children to track their reading over a period of time and enable them to discover trends in their own reading habits. Their reading can easily span the curriculum. Nonfiction offers a wealth of choices for children to pick from in pursuing a special interest generated either in or out of school. Fiction can provide strong factual content as authors establish settings and develop characters. And, of course, literature is important in its own right as children read for enjoyment.

4 WRITERS' NOTEBOOKS are places to store our ideas—from the profound to the quirky. James Moffett, internationally known for his lifetime of work in language arts instruction and curriculum development, effectively summarizes convincing reasons for keeping a writer's notebook: "The best writing stimuli are our own feelings, memories, sensations, reflections, and imaginings. But these are often fleeting, and unless we note some of them down, we may not recover them.

That is why so many professional writers keep notebooks to record these in whatever form they occur" (Moffett, 1992, 211).

What Makes a Good Journal?

Every good teacher is aware of children's individuality; each child's journal will be unique, too. Nevertheless, good journals share a number of characteristics. They are apt to be conversational, peppered with first-person pronouns, marked by the rhythms of everyday speech, and various—as the writer tries out different writing styles and formats (Fulwiler, 1987). Fulwiler also notes that journals serve their purpose when they are rich in these qualities:

Observations: *For personal reasons and to enhance school learning, it is important to notice things. Making observations is vital to the work of the scientist, but it is equally important to the writer, the artist, the historian, and the mathematician.*

Questions: *Questions reveal a mind at work. Questions guide observation. Questions organize projects. Questions test conclusions. Questions remind us what we want to find out.*

Speculations: *Journals are places in which writers wonder about ideas, events, issues, and problems.*

Evidence of developing self-awareness: *By writing, and by reading what they have written over time, writers develop a sense of who they are, what they believe in, and what makes them unique.*

Digressions: *Writers should feel free to change directions, make new connections, elaborate points, and raise counterexamples, following their thinking wherever it leads them.*

Synthesis: *Journals enable writers to put ideas and information together in new ways, juxtaposing one thing and another, even when the connection between them has yet to be made explicit.*

Revisions: *Journals are places to try things out; journal writers may change their minds, revising an idea or scrapping it in favor of something new.*

Information: *Some learning does depend on outside sources—classroom experiences, readings, the advice of peers, and so on. Journal entries can help children take in outside information.*

Is There Enough Time for Journal Writing?

Time allocated for journal writing is not time taken away from other subjects. Just the opposite! It is time needed for basic instruction—time identified and reserved for children's engagement with inquiry activity in science, social studies, mathematics, and literature. Consequently, the importance of journal writing should be reflected routinely in the class schedule.

Understandably, each teacher must decide  what is most appropriate for his/her classroom. The exact number of minutes allocated to journal writing will vary depending on children's experiences (they will need more time if they are just learning to use their journals), on what they are studying, and on their interests and abilities. But even with all of these variables, journal writing should be a part of each day's instructional schedule. Journal activity is trivialized when it is used as a time-filler or "sponge" activity to quiet children down after recess or lunch.

As children become increasingly proficient at using their journals—making entries and applying the entries to their work in subject areas—they may do some journal work outside the classroom. This capacity for independent work is certainly a worthwhile objective. However, remember that the journals discussed here are learning tools, not personal diaries; their place in the classroom remains important.

As important as journal writing is, teachers should not lose sight of the value of "just reading." Children need ample time to write, but they also need time to read, perhaps just browse. Why? An increasing number of research studies show that "just reading," or reading without any attendant pre-reading or post-reading activities, is a powerful tool for improving reading skills (Pearson, 1993, 508). "Just reading," moreover, helps children relax and enjoy books in the way that literate adults do. Children should also have options after they read, including the option of simply putting the book away. Too many activities can quickly dull the enthusiasm generated by a "good read."

What About Grades?

Most everyone agrees that journal entries should not be formally evaluated in the way worksheets or finished compositions are. For journals to be effective, children need to feel free to experiment with what and how they write. Journals, logs, and notebooks are the places for children to stretch and grow as learners—taking chances, exploring new ground, trying ideas they might not have the courage to vocalize or write down on a test or in a composition. However, both children and teachers may need some convincing that journal writing is important even if it isn't graded. Children may even benefit from incentives to help them learn how journal activities contribute directly to their overall efforts in mathematics, literature, science, and social studies, as well as to the development of their writing skills. Consider the following among the possibilities:

■ Teachers can scan journal entries periodically simply by walking about in the classroom to record occasional marks of "✓" or "−," indicating whether children have or have not participated in selected journal activities. In other words, children would get credit simply for participating in journal writing, and lose credit if they do not. The record of these notations could be weighed in the total profile of each student's achievement record just as other measures are (such as homework completion, for example).

■ In each marking period, teachers may use selected journal activities as initial steps (or "scaffolding") toward completion of a project (like a speech, a simulation, a skit, or a paper) that is graded. In other words, children would need to rely on journal activities such as collecting data, making observations, recording interview notes, organizing information, and writing drafts, to produce a final project. The grade on the final project could include some points allocated for good work on the journal activity associated with it, in the same way mathematics teachers give credit to students who do a good job of "showing their work" in arriving at the answer to a problem.

■ As they relate specifically to instruction in composition, journal entries can be evaluated as steps in process writing—the prewriting, drafting, and revising stages in the process of working up a final draft. Since final drafts are likely to be graded, good work done on the journal activity helps students do well on the final project. Here, too, the final grade could allocate some points or credit for the journal activity associated with it.

■ Certain subject matter tests and quizzes could be given as "open journal" tests and quizzes. The test in this case could be written to include some questions related to content addressed recently in journal activities. Children who had informative and easily accessible journal entries would have an advantage. This use of journals resembles the use adults make of reference materials in their work.

■ Teachers could review journals with children during student/teacher conferences. Instances of good journal work, including improvement, could be cited, as could patterns of non-completion.

■ Similarly, teachers could review students' journals with parents at parent conference time.

What About Punctuation and Spelling?

Journal writing should not be used as a means to teach punctuation and spelling. Instead, journals help children to compose their thoughts and ideas without slowing down to worry about how they have transcribed them. Children should concentrate on content rather than transcription, sharing their entries and using them as stepping stones to other projects.

If children do extend themselves and take some chances, they will make spelling and punctuation errors, since they are likely to use words and syntactic patterns they haven't mastered yet. These errors can inform teachers about what to address in the portion of their language arts program given over to the teaching of transcription

skills. In other words, journals need not displace the teaching of skills, and skills teaching should not displace journal writing. The two learning strategies can complement each other.

What About Privacy?

Whenever educators get together to discuss the use of journals, questions arise about student privacy. Some arise because parents object to school assignments that seem to them to intrude on family matters. Others acknowledge that some students respond uneasily to assignments calling for introspection and self-disclosure. Still others are prompted by students who respond too eagerly, using school assignments to upstage others who are more reticent. These are serious issues; our convictions about the importance of journal writing should not cause us to dismiss them.

However, the journal writing activities in *Writing Journals* are not intended to be intrusive. They are not intended as vehicles for counseling; that is a separate domain. Rather, they are directly related to curricular study. But, how do teachers engage children in direct, searching written work without invading their privacy? The following suggestions are drawn from "Guidelines for Using Journals in School Settings," approved by the NCTE (National Council of Teachers of English) Commission on Composition:

■ Explain that a journal is a place to write about things related in one way or another to the content of a particular area of study.

■ Encourage children to use looseleaf notebooks (folders could also be used). This allows a child to remove any entries which s/he does not wish others to see.

■ Suggest that children divide their journals into sections (or keep multiple journals). That way, only the section that bears on what is being studied or shared needs to be publicly available.

What About Journals and the Bilingual Student?

Children who are just beginning to speak and read in English learn most quickly when they are engaged in real communicative exchanges about personal, concrete experiences. Here, too, journals can play an important role. "A journal kept by a bilingual student...can provide the teacher with valuable insights into the student and the learning process. Journals provide a personal glimpse of each student's feelings and emotions and are a window to each student's progress" (Farris and Cooper, 1994, 274).

Writing Journals presents many activities that ask students to respond personally to what they encounter in the classroom and in their readings. *Writing Journals* also emphasizes cooperative learning. Certainly these strategies are sound for all students, both for those who have spoken English all their lives and for those who are learning it now.

What About Computers?

More and more computers and software programs are available to students and teachers. As computer technology expands, the costs of hardware and software are decreasing. Consequently, children in some schools may be able to keep their journals and logs in computer files. But no matter how many computers are available in your classroom, they probably aren't portable. Children can't take them home at night, or tuck them under their arms on field trips or

during a session at the library. That's why even in this electronic age there is still an important role for portable journals of the paper-and-pen variety.

Journals and computers can be brought together easily in the classroom as children re-work their writing from one stage to another in a composing process. With the help of a number of software programs children can experiment with different writing formats—newspapers, books, research reports, and so on—and give them a professional look. Program spell-checkers and an on-line thesaurus are useful to all young writers. With this powerful set of tools, children can use their journal entries as the basis for creating a wide variety of writing projects, to be published and then read by many audiences.

NOTE: A listing of several appropriate software programs for children in grades four to six appears on page 138. It should be noted that this list is not comprehensive and, given our climate of rapid technological development, it will not stay current. New programs are being developed even as *Writing Journals* goes to press.

A Few More Words About Dialogue Journals

Because dialogue journals have a place in all curricular areas, let's discuss them here rather than in each of the separate subject sections of *Writing Journals.* The best way to describe a dialogue journal is to liken it to a conversation. Here, the conversational partners are a teacher and a student, and the journal is a place to talk, in writing, about subjects of mutual interest. Dialogue journals foster communication. They encourage children to express themselves to their teachers in thoughtful, informal ways. These interchanges benefit teachers, too, enabling them to gain new insights into their students. And, while learning to understand children's interests, curiosities, and concerns, teachers have opportunities to share something of themselves.

Unlike the other journals we discuss in *Writing Journals,* dialogue journals are not shared; they are exchanged only by the conversation partners. Nevertheless, their purpose is not to offer personal counsel. Rather, dialogue journals have a functional nature. Staton (1987, 49-52) points to four specific purposes:

Requesting information: *Could you help me figure out how to divide fractions? I still don't understand.*

Promising: *I know I said I would work on extra credit problems in math, and I haven't. I'll really try to do some next week.*

Giving directions: *Would you remember to teach us that folk song about Madeline, the Paddlin' Fool?*

Offering: *I know you like books about horses. I just read one by Marguerite Henry that was great. I'll lend it to you if you want me to.*

Dialogue journals are interactive—students and teachers comment on one another's entries. But while both partners are readers and writers, it is the teacher's enthusiasm for the project that is critical to its success.

Typical entries are brief, since children are encouraged to write at any time during the school day when something that interests or concerns them comes up. The teacher's response should be positive, encouraging, and about as long as the child's entry. Rather than asking questions, urge children to elaborate on their comments and add interesting information about the topics they bring up.

Dialogue journals require patience. It will probably take time to develop the habit of writing in dialogue journals for both you and your students. The following are based on tips that Staton has found helpful in launching and then fostering this special kind of communication:

■ Talk with children about why people need to communicate with each other. Urge them to think about all the times when conversation is essential. Also think of times when we talk with others just because it's enjoyable. With this as background, introduce the dialogue journal as a written conversation.

■ Emphasize that only two people will see the journal—the two writers.

■ List some starter topics: opinions on the lunch program, requests for help in a particular subject, complaints about the vacation schedule, suggestions for class field trips, etc. After the routine is established, let children take the lead in initiating topics.

■ Reassure children that their entries won't be graded and they don't need to be any particular length.

■ Establish an agreed-upon way to exchange journals so that privacy is maintained.

Every aspect of the curriculum provides appropriate subjects for dialogue journals. Children and teachers can talk together about what is being studied as well as how it is being learned. They can share ideas, encouragements and complaints. Individual entries will almost certainly be various. But, when taken together, they are likely to reveal the development of mutual respect between teacher and learner in the school community.

Getting Started

"And so as teachers we walk a thin line. We want to suggest possibilities for using notebooks, but we also want to give youngsters the space to invent their own" (Calkins, 1991, 51).

The children in your classroom have their journals, looseleaf notebooks or pocket folders in their desks. What's next? How do you establish journal writing as a classroom routine? How do you sustain interest? How do you ensure that children have a sense of ownership in what they write? Here are some approaches.

The Teacher as a Model

The example you set—as an adult who is a writer—will influence your success in sponsoring journal writing in your classroom. Keep your own journals, write in them as your class writes, and share your entries just as you ask children to share theirs. Your commitment to journal writing will not be lost on the children. The fact that you are a participant will validate the project in the children's eyes. Moreover, you will give children an example to follow in writing journal entries of their own.

You might begin a journal-writing activity by reading aloud a journal entry that you have written in advance. Say, perhaps, that you are asking children to search their memories for remembrances of one sort or another: of times when they felt courageous or afraid, of people who made impressions on them, of travels to new places, etc. Share what you have written about a memorable experience of your own. Here, for example, is a journal entry, made by a teacher

during a summertime canoe trip in northeastern Minnesota, which she shared with her class:

"Today, the 8th day on trail, was our first layover day and it couldn't have come at a better time. We're camped at a nice spot on Sturgeon Lake, and we've spent the whole day cooking, baking, eating, washing clothes, greasing boots and reading The Singing Wilderness. *Now there is a 3/4 moon in the sky, so I guess in a few nights we'll have quite a sight in store for us. It's amazing how the moon can add so much light to these otherwise dark woods. Altogether, what a beautiful day this has been."*

Perhaps what you have written will be a list, a chronology, or a short piece focused on one person or event. In any case, show children how you have used your journal pages as working pages—crossing out words, reordering phrases, or even whole sentences or paragraphs. Ask them to comment on what you have written and encourage questions. With experiences like this as background, children have a better understanding of how to go about writing in their own journals.

Launching a New Area of Study

Here is an ideal starting point for journal use: launching a new unit with a journal-writing activity. Following are two strategies. In one, you can begin by asking children to write down everything they think they know about the topic to be studied. Alternatively, ask them to write down what their expectations are for the new unit. What do they want to learn? What do they think they actually will learn?

Asking children to respond to prompts like these draws them into the study that is to follow. Their entries should inform your teaching approaches, as well. You can gain important insights into how much the children actually do know about a topic and adjust your instruction accordingly.

For example, consider how the following entry tells us how much Amanda already knows about winter, and what topics her teacher might develop as the class begins a new unit on the seasons:

> *"There is quite a bit to tell when winter is coming. Here are some good reasons.*
>
> 1. *All kinds of birds go south.*
> 2. *It starts to get dark early.*
> 3. *It gets alot colder too!*
> 4. *Some animals go into hibernation.*
> 5. *The leaves start to lose their leaves.*
> 6. *Also by when the holidays come.*
> 7. *Snow starts to fall.*
> 8. *You have to dress warm.*
> 9. *Deer HUNTING tells me.*
> 10. *That's all I know for now."*

Journal entries can continue to be useful throughout a unit of study. For example, consider compiling what children have written onto a class chart for reference throughout the course of study. Were children's assumptions about a topic borne out by their study? What proved to be incorrect? What new information was added? Children's journal entries about what they hope to learn in a new unit can become the basis for establishing a set of objectives for study, a kind of road map for the class and individual work that follows. Either way, children will immediately see that their journal entries are put to use—that they count for something. This principle of using journal entries as stepping stones for sharing, for

learning, and for future writing guides all of the suggestions in *Writing Journals*.

Beginning with Personal Experiences

We tend to do our best writing on the things we know the most about. Apply that understanding to children's early experiences with journal writing. Journal prompts that ask children to recall their own experiences make first entries easier. For example, let's consider prompts related to school experiences as examples of how to get children started. What do children see on the bus ride or their walk to school every day? Is the bus ride fun or tiresome? Is the walk enjoyable or worrisome? What about the classroom itself? How could the learning center be made more interesting and/or accessible? When should recess be scheduled? What's the best time for math—morning or afternoon? The lists of possibilities, both in topics and in writing prompts, are long ones, and they can be adapted specifically to your own classroom situation. The only important point here relates to selection: the first topics you choose should be those that everyone in your class will have had experience with and an opinion about. In the following example, a fourth-grade teacher asked children to write a journal entry about the biggest mess they ever made, an excellent starter. Who doesn't have something to say? Sydney responded with:

> *"The biggest mess I ever made was when my mom and I were making Christmas cookies. I was going to get the sugar so I hopped up on the counter and I opened the cupboard and I grabbed the handle of the cover that covered the container that the sugar was in. As I lifted it out and POP! the cover came off and sugar went everywhere. I'm lucky my*

From *Writing Journals*, published by GoodYearBooks. Copyright © 1996 Linda Western.

mom didn't get that mad like she was going to explode. But she did get mad. We could save a little of it, but not all of it. The bad part was that my mom had to clean up. I helped a little."

As your students write, be sure to write yourself. Share your views. If students' entries contain suggestions for how something might be improved, look together to see whether those ideas might be acted upon.

NOTE: See pages 11–12 on dialogue journals for further discussion about children's journal writing and school activities.

From *Writing Journals*, published by GoodYearBooks. Copyright © 1996 Linda Western.

Pointing to Others Who Have Kept Journals

 In addition to showing children your own journals, tell them about others who valued journal writing. Your examples may be historical figures. Lewis and Clark, Thomas Edison, George Washington, and Leonardo Da Vinci are among the many who kept some sort of journal. Still other examples can come from literature. *A Gathering of Days: A New England Girl's Journal, 1830-1832,* by Joan Blos (1979), offers readers a unique perspective on life in early America. In contrast, Louise Fitzhugh's *Harriet the Spy* (1964) has a contemporary setting. Readers learn about the complicated Harriet, in part, through her journal writings. Some authors of children's books are journal writers, too. Jane Yolen is one. In one of her favorite anecdotes, she tells the story of hearing an advertisement for a fence on the radio: it was "horse-high, hog-tight, and bull-strong." Fascinated by the words, she recorded them in her notebook, and used them much later in the first paragraph of *The Inway Investigators:* "What makes a good fence? Grandad used to say being 'horse-high, hog-tight,

and bull-strong.'" (Unfortunately, this book, published in 1973, is now out of print; however, the original edition may still be in your library.)

You may want to draw on examples reprinted in sources written for teachers, such as Nancie Atwell's *Coming to Know: Writing to Learn in the Intermediate Grades* (1990), and Lucy Calkins' *Living Between the Lines* (1991). Perhaps you will want to draw on examples written by children in your district or even in your own school. Clearly, however, the most relevant examples will be the writings of the children in your class.

Helping Children to See Why Journal Writing Is Important

Writer after writer on the topic of journal writing points to the importance of providing children with opportunities to use their journal writings in other contexts—in projects that they choose to pursue and see as meaningful.

■ *Sharing entries is central to this effort.* Just as you set aside time each day so that children can write in their journals, provide time for them to tell others what they have written.

■ *Encourage children to refer to their entries in discussion.* Though Moffett and Wagner speak to this point in the context of reader response journals, their finding can be broadly applied: "The habit of keeping the journals will improve discussion enormously when students need to talk about a text...they extract or paraphrase ideas from these reading records and then respond to each other's responses" (Moffett & Wagner, 162).

■ *Use journal entries as the launching points for new activities.* When children draw on what they have written—revising material, reordering it, supplementing it with new writing, seeing the need for further research and writing, and then moving on to a project they have identified as being important—the usefulness of journals will be clear in their own eyes. "If teachers and children are not pursuing their writing beyond the level of collecting entries, then there is often no reason to confer, no need for share sessions, no occasions for revision, no intention to craft literature, no opportunity to make reading-writing connections..." (Calkins, 82).

■ *Show children how their journals also serve as records of personal growth and development.* Their entries in learning logs, for example, can show children not only what but how they are learning. Dialogue journal entries remind them of how they felt about the learning process: what was easy, what was hard, and how their teachers offered encouragement and tips. Reader response journals not only help children remember their reactions to particular books, they also provide an ongoing record of what children have read during a given period of time. And a writer's notebook can be an incubator for writing projects in the future.

The following is a partial listing of stories that include letters, journals, or diaries as a significant element in character and/or plot development:

Blos, J. (1979). *A Gathering of Days: A New England Girl's Journal*, 1830-1832. New York: Macmillan.

Brison, P. (1989). *Your Best Friend, Kate.* (R. Brown, Illus.) New York: Macmillan.

Casely, J. (1991). *Dear Annie.* New York: Greenwillow.

Cleary, B. (1983). *Dear Mr. Henshaw.* (P. O. Zelinsky, Illus.) New York: Morrow Junior Books.

Colman, Hila. (1985). *Diary of a Frantic Kid Sister.* New York: Simon & Schuster, Inc.

Fitzhugh, L. (1964). *Harriet the Spy.* New York: HarperCollins.

Frank, A. (1967). *Ann Frank: The Diary of a Young Girl.* (B.M. Mooyaart, Trans.) New York: Doubleday.

Giff, P. R. (1991). *The War Began at Supper: Letters to Miss Loria.* New York: Dell.

MacLachlan, P. (1985). *Sarah, Plain and Tall.* New York: HarperCollins.

Moore, I. (1991). *Little Dog Lost.* New York: Macmillan.

Turner, A. (1987). *Nettie's Trip South.* (R. Himler, Illus.) New York: Macmillan.

Va, Leong. (1991). *A Letter to the King.* (J. Anderson, Trans.) New York: HarperCollins.

Williams, V. B. (1988). *Stringbean's Trip to the Shining Sea.* (J. Williams, Illus.) New York: Greenwillow.

From *Writing Journals*, published by GoodYearBooks. Copyright © 1996 Linda Western.

Journal Writing and Literature

An Overview

Learning Logs

OBSERVATIONS AND INTERACTIONS

Fact or Fantasy?

Comparing What We Know with What We Read

New Times and New Places: The Information We Can Learn from Fiction

What Does It Take to Be a Main Character?

Developing an Understanding of Folklore and the Oral Tradition

EXPLORATION AND RESEARCH

Getting to Know You, Getting to Know All About You: Character Development in Fiction

Once Upon a Time: A Familiar Story Pattern

What's the Problem Here? Recognizing Conflict Patterns in Stories

Plot and Theme—What's the Difference?

Learning More About Authors and Illustrators

Discovering Poetic Conventions

Reader Response Journals

OBSERVATIONS AND INTERACTIONS

Making Predictions

What Sort of Place Is This? Settings That Create Moods

Noticing How Characters Change

What Would I Do in a Situation Like That?

What Makes a Book Funny?

Clues in Illustrations

EXPLORATION AND RESEARCH

What Kind of Mystery Do You Like? Creating a Survey

This Story (Poem) Reminds Me of...

Which Version Do I Like Best?

Tell It to the Judge

Remembering Special Poems

Discovering Personal Reading Preferences

Writers' Notebooks

OBSERVATIONS AND INTERACTIONS

Consider the Source: Exploring Point of View

A Penny for Your Thoughts: Writing a Character's Diary

Advice to an Author

Let Me Tell You Why We Say That!

Writing a Character Biography

Writing Poetry

EXPLORATION AND RESEARCH

Creating a Fanciful Character

Writing an Original Myth

Planning a Sequel

Changing Genres—Poetry to Prose (and Vice Versa!)

Jokes, Riddles, and Word Play

Play Making

References

Children's Books Referred to in This Section

Sources on Book Making

From *Writing Journals*, published by GoodYearBooks. Copyright © 1996 Linda Western.

Overview

Reading and writing are natural partners. Because of the range and quality of stories and poetry written for children, literature study is an ideal arena for engaging children in meaningful writing activities. However, we should remember that just because children like to read stories doesn't necessarily mean that they enjoy writing about them. (The words "book report" probably still conjure up unpleasant memories for many of us!)

The activities in the literature section of *Writing Journals* are a far cry from book reports. Instead, we will be exploring how enjoyment and understanding of literature can be enhanced when reading and journal writing follow in meaningful ways from each other.

Why incorporate journal writing in children's literature study? Consider these reasons:

- ■ Entries can be in direct response to children's interests and preferences. As children note what they have enjoyed or disliked about a book, as they react to characters and settings, as they evaluate the abilities of authors and illustrators to capture their attention, they can jot down their thoughts. Over time, these entries can serve as a tangible record of reading progress and help children discover patterns in what they have chosen to read.

- ■ Journals can be a practice ground as children learn how to talk about literature. Children can initiate their own writing or they can respond to prompts. They also can write in response to direct instruction. In *Writing Journals,* several writing activities follow from teacher-led lessons designed to heighten understanding of literary elements.

- ■ Journal entries can serve as the basis for discussions about what has been read as well as a launching point for further reading and study.

- ■ Journal entries can provide the seeds for further writing activities.

Even though the following activities are all related in one way or another to literature study, their purposes vary. Some are designed to lead children in learning more about literature, its genres and elements. Others should help children explore their own reading interests as well as those of others. Still others are intended to guide children toward making informed evaluations of what they read and write.

Further, these activities suggest ways for children to use three types of journals: learning logs, reader response journals, and writers' notebooks. A fourth, the dialogue journal, also lends itself well to literature study. Dialogue journals are discussed on pages 11–12.

These suggestions for each type of journal are placed in two categories. Those listed under **Observations and Interactions** engage children in journal writing that draws on what they already know or can learn from their immediate surroundings—home, school and community. Those listed under the heading **Exploration and Research** cause children to widen their focus as they explore others' ideas, gather new information, engage in instructional experiences where the outcome is unknown, and practice applying what they have learned.

Please consider these suggestions as a kind of smorgasbord. Choose those that are best suited to both your instructional objectives and to the

From *Writing Journals,* published by GoodYearBooks. Copyright © 1996 Linda Western.

interests of your students. Also, remember that all of the following suggestions for journal writing are intended to lead to further study: more reading, writing, investigation, or discussion. Encourage children to share what they have written and help them use their entries in additional activities that they will see as purposeful.

Learning Logs

OBSERVATIONS AND INTERACTIONS

◢ Fact or Fantasy?

Stories of fantasy tell of things that cannot exist outside our imagination: animals talk, people travel through time, spells are cast. In contrast, realistic fiction tells of what has happened or could happen. Children can use their learning logs as they read to discover this important distinction in literary genres.

Ask your school librarian to gather together a wide selection of fantasy stories. Read one aloud and talk with children about which elements of the story could really happen and which ones could not. Then, make two columns on the chalkboard, labeling one **Imaginary**, the other **Real.** Ask children to take turns entering elements from the story—characters, setting, action, etc.—into the appropriate column. (The example below is based on E. B. White's *Charlotte's Web* [1952].) Refer to the chart you have made together

Figure 1

Imaginary	Real
Animals speak to each other as humans do	Animals live in a farmyard just as real animals do
Fern can hear the animals speak	The other human characters can't hear the animals speak
Charlotte is able to weave words into her webs	Real spiders create webs and catch insects in them just as Charlotte does
Wilbur, Charlotte, and Templeton have many of the same feelings as humans	Charlotte's life cycle is like that of real spiders

as you explain the distinction that sets fantasy apart from realistic fiction.

Next, invite children to select stories they would like to read. After they have made their selections, ask them to divide a page from their learning logs into two columns in order to make a chart like the one you have made together on the chalkboard. Then, as they read, ask children to notice what is real and what is imaginary in their stories, filling in the columns accordingly.

After children have completed their reading, spend time sharing observations. You may want to create a master list on the chalkboard to display the imaginary elements the children have discovered.

From *Writing Journals*, published by GoodYearBooks. Copyright © 1996 Linda Western.

EXTENSION:

If fantasy stories tell of things that aren't real, why do people read them? Engage children in a discussion about authors' abilities to make their stories of fantasy interesting or believable. Were children persuaded to accept the characters and the plot of the story they just read? Why or why not? Would they like to read other stories by the same author? Would they like to read other stories of fantasy? Remind children to look back at their journal entries as they answer these questions.

Comparing What We Know with What We Read

All of us tend to read with special interest when we can relate our own experiences to what we are reading. This activity is designed to facilitate making this kind of connection. Help children to find a book set in a location they are familiar with. It might be urban—the Mexican-American neighborhood in Gary Soto's *Local News* (1993), for example; or a farm, as in Patricia MacLachlan's *Arthur, for the Very First Time* (1980);

or a rural setting, like the one in Katherine Paterson's *Bridge to Terabithia* (1977); or perhaps even an area vulnerable to a particular kind of weather pattern, as in Ivy Ruckman's *Night of the Twisters* (1984), set in central Nebraska.

As they read, ask children to use their learning logs to note how the settings of their stories remind them of where they live. What are the differences? Ask them to tell, using their own experiences as benchmarks, whether or not the author has been successful in conveying to readers what life on a farm, in a city, on the seacoast, in the mountains, and so on, could be like. Help them to discover that their entries can form the basis of meaningful evaluations of what they have read. Provide time for children to share these evaluations with the rest of the class.

EXTENSION:

Children could note suggestions for how the author might have developed an added sense of setting for readers. What situations might the characters have experienced? What other descriptions could have been included? Encourage children to use these notes in drafting a paragraph (or more if they wish) that could be added to the book.

New Times and New Places: The Information We Can Learn from Fiction

Many stories for children develop settings that are likely to be new to them. In historical fiction, both time and place will be unfamiliar. In contemporary fiction, the place can easily be unknown. This learning log activity helps children to see how they can learn a great deal about other times and other places through the stories they read.

Begin by asking children to make two columns on a page in their learning logs. Before they start to read, ask them to use the first column to list everything they already know about the setting in the book they have chosen (for example colonial America, life today in New York City, and so on). Then, as they read, ask children to use the second column to write down what they learn about that setting from the story.

Encourage children to make comparisons between the entries in the two columns as they read. Questions that could prompt discussion and evaluation include: Am I learning anything new about a different time and/or place? How is this information presented? Is the author verifying the information I already have? Has the author contradicted something I said? Am I confident that the author is correct?

From *Writing Journals*, published by GoodYearBooks. Copyright © 1996 Linda Western.

This reading may prompt children to choose another book with a similar setting (another work of fiction or a nonfiction account) so that they can continue to cross-check information.

What Does It Take to Be a Main Character?

Ask children to think about the main character in a story they are reading. What makes this character stand out from the others? Ask children to make a list in their learning logs of what they think qualifies this character to be the main character.

Now you can pose a question. Do these lists settle the issue of what sets a main character apart

from the rest? Children can find out by checking their lists against the next books they read. How do the new characters they are reading about measure up to the characteristics on their lists? Is there anything that should be added? changed? Are there differences because of the kind of story the characters appear in? Children's expanded lists should be the basis for class or small group discussions as they make comparisons. Remind children how much they can learn from each other and encourage them to continue to edit and add to their lists during these interchanges of ideas.

EXTENSION:

Now the children are in a good position to imagine a main character they would like to create. Using the ideas they have developed above, they could plan how they would introduce that character and develop a story around him/her. Plans should be shared, and perhaps taken one step further as children actually write their own stories.

Developing an Understanding of Folklore and the Oral Tradition

The genre of folklore includes folk tales, fables, myths, and legends. For centuries throughout the world these stories were passed along to new generations by storytellers. This telling of stories is known as *oral tradition*. We have access to folklore today because of the work of collectors, translators, and adaptors—all writers who captured these stories and put them on paper.

Children are participants in an oral tradition, too, though they probably don't know that they are. You can help them learn about their own oral tradition through this learning log activity.

Ask children to recall chants they may have used in playing games ("Red Rover, Red Rover" or "Moonlight, Starlight," for example), or chants from jump-rope rhymes ("Teddy Bear, Teddy Bear, Turn Around. . ."). Arrange for the children to perform some of these chants in class so that the memory of them will come alive. Then ask the children to record the chants in their learning logs—explaining that this is what collectors of folk tales do to make sure that old stories don't disappear from memory.

Children can follow the same practice to record stories they have heard family members tell—the ones that are told over and over again. Family stories are important to children. They answer children's curiosity about basic questions of identity: Who am I? Where did I come from? How did I get to be where I am now?

Later, after they have had time to gather their stories, ask children to share with the class what they have recorded. In your discussion, help children to realize that all of us know family stories, as well as chants and rhymes, even though we have never read them anywhere. We know them because we have listened to others. The oral tradition in contemporary society is still alive and well!

NOTE: To help children get started, consider exploring the verses and illustrations in Jane Yolen's *Street Rhymes Around the World* (1992), which includes 32 songs and chants from 17 nations and republics. You might also want to show children the books of Richard Chase (*The Jack Tales* [1943]), for example. Chase includes notes on the sources of the stories he has retold.

EXTENSION:

Children can extend their survey of childhood rhymes and chants by asking parents and grandparents what chants they remember from their childhood games. Children may be surprised to learn about the continuity of the oral tradition across generations.

This activity provides yet another extension possibility. Notes on often-told family stories can provide the framework for written stories. (Authors often incorporate real episodes from family stories into their plots.) Children can either write their families' favorite stories essentially as they are told, or they can embellish them. A collection of these stories would make a fine addition to your classroom library.

From *Writing Journals*, published by GoodYearBooks. Copyright © 1996 Linda Western.

Getting to Know You, Getting to Know All About You: Character Development in Fiction

We learn about characters in stories through what they do, say, and think; we also learn about them from the narrator and by what other characters say of them. Discovering how authors develop characterizations builds children's understanding of literature and can help them with their own writing.

Pose a question to your class. "When you finish reading a story you like, do you feel familiar with the characters in it?" Children probably do come away from their reading with a definite sense of what at least some characters are like. But how can this be? They've never really met these characters. How did they get to know them? To begin answering this question, ask the children to make a chart like the one on page 24 (Figure 2) in their learning logs—filling it in, wherever appropriate, as they search through a story they have just read.

Ask children to use their chart entries as they talk together about the books they have read. Are some approaches to developing characterization used more than others? How successful have these authors been in helping readers feel they know the characters?

EXTENSION:

Ask children to read another book by the same author and fill out a new chart about its main character. Does the author rely on the same techniques in the second book? Do the characters in the second book seem similar to those in the first? What are the differences?

Once Upon a Time: A Familiar Story Pattern

A study of literary elements can be an exciting one when it grows out of children's discoveries. In this learning log activity, children can discover for themselves the pattern that we see in so many folk tales: typed characters; vague settings; a rapid introduction of the problem that often involves a search against great odds for food, money, a companion, or security; a resolution to the problem; and a brief conclusion.

Begin by reading two or three folk tales aloud to children. Work together to fill in a chart, like the one on page 25 (Figure 3), which you have written on the chalkboard. Lead children in seeing that we rarely learn very much about any of the characters: they are usually only good or bad, kind or evil. Nor do we know much about when or where the story happens. The problem the characters face is typically introduced immediately. When the problem is resolved, the story quickly ends. This is a common formula for folk tales. Though the details of the stories vary, the pattern in which they unfold is remarkably predictable.

Now children are ready to explore some folk tales on their own. Ask them to create a similar chart in their logs and fill it in as they read. Encourage them to share their completed charts and show others the books they used in making the comparisons.

Characterization Chart

Figure 2

Name _____ Date _____

Characterization chart for _____

in _____ by _____

Technique	Observations	Pages where examples can be found
Based on what the character says, I think s/he is		
Based on what the character thinks, I think s/he is		
Based on what the character does, I think s/he is		
Based on what others say about the character, I think s/he is		
Based on what the narrator says about the character, I think s/he is		

From *Writing Journals*, published by GoodYearBooks. Copyright © 1996 Linda Western.

Comparing Three Tales

	Version A	Version B	Version C	Similarities	Differences	Conclusions
CHARACTERS	Cinderella: good and beautiful. Her 2 stepsisters: mean and nasty. Her stepmother: cruel. Her father: afraid of his wife. Godmother: magical. Prince: rich.	Nomi: good and beautiful. Her 1 stepsister: unimportant to the story. Her stepmother: cruel. Fish: magical. Dog: loyal but unwise. Chief: rich.	Maria: good and beautiful. Her stepmother: cruel. Her stepsister: we know little about her. Crab and crocodile: magical. Tree: magical. Old woman: magical. King: rich	Cinderella, Nomi and Maria all are good and beautiful. Each one marries someone rich. Each one has a cruel stepmother. Each story has at least one magical being.	The number and kind of magical creatures varies. The number of stepsisters varies. Maria's father is cruel, Cinderella's father is afraid, and Nomi's father is unimportant to the story.	We can describe every character with one or two words: good, evil, kind, etc.
SETTING	Unclear. We know little about where Cinderella lives. We know only that the prince lives in a castle.	Unclear. We know only that Nomi lives near the veld. We know only that the Chief lives at the Great Palace.	Unclear. We know only that Maria lives in a house near the river. We know only that the king lives in a palace.	Cinderella, Nomi and Maria all live in houses, but we know nothing about what each house is like. The prince, Chief and king all live in a grand palace, but again, we know little what each palace is like.	Nomi lives near a veld and Maria lives near a river.	We don't know when any of the stories took place. We know very little about where they took place.
PROBLEM	We learn immediately that Cinderella is badly treated by her stepmother and stepsisters (page 1, paragraph 2).	We learn immediately that Nomi is badly treated by her stepmother (page 1, paragraph 3).	We learn immediately that Maria is badly treated by her stepmother (page 1, paragraph 1).	Cinderella, Nomi and Maria all are badly treated. All three are overworked. All are confronted by someone more powerful.	Besides being overworked, Nomi does not have enough to eat. Maria's father also is cruel.	We learn about the main characters' problems on the first page. Cinderella, Nomi and Maria have no one to help them except a magical being.
ENDING	Cinderella's foot easily fits into the slipper. She marries the prince. She forgives her stepsisters.	Only Nomi is able to pick up the bones. The Chief promises to marry her. Her stepmother and stepsister run away.	Maria's foot fits easily into the slipper. She and the king are happy together.	Cinderella, Maria and Nomi live happily ever after.	Cinderella forgives her stepsisters. Nomi's mother and stepsister run away. We don't know what happens to Maria's stepmother.	The stories all end as soon as the couples are united. The "good" main character (Cinderella, Nomi, Maria) is rewarded with riches.

From *Writing Journals*, published by GoodYearBooks. Copyright © 1996 Linda Western.

Journal Writing and Literature 25

Children can use this technique in discovering this folk tale pattern at work in other tales from many different cultures. They could also enjoy studying variations of one tale. The chart on p. 25 is based on three versions of Cinderella—there are reported to be 1,500 versions of this tale alone! These three, however, are found in The Oryx Multicultural Folktale Series: Cinderella *(1992), compiled by Judy Sierra, which contains retellings of 25 Cinderella stories. Version A is the familiar "Cinderella, or the Little Glass Slipper" (French); Version B is "Nomi and The Magic Fish," told by the Zulu; and Version C is "Maria," a tale from the Philippines. References to additional variants are found on page 79.*

What's the Problem Here? Recognizing Conflict Patterns in Stories

Virtually every story involves some kind of conflict; we catch hints of it early on, and we keep reading to find out how it will be resolved. The conflict may pit the main character against another person, against society, against nature, or against himself/herself.

Some stories focus on one main conflict. For example, throughout the pages of Mary Rodgers' *Freaky Friday* (1972), Annabel struggles, often humorously, with herself as she discovers how others see her. In others, more than one conflict is developed. In Jean Craighead George's *Julie of the Wolves* (1974), Julie struggles against her arranged marriage and all the constraints of life in a small, remote settlement. She leaves her home only to fight for survival on the harsh tundra. But she also must deal with the changes in the Arctic

wrought by modernization. Most importantly, she must deal with her own attitudes about those changes, since they threaten the sense she has developed of her own identity.

You can help children to recognize these four kinds of conflict that appear, alone or in combination, in story after story. Noticing a conflict while reading helps all readers read. We read, then, with anticipation.

Begin by basing your discussion on a book you are reading to the class. Talk together about the conflict(s) the author develops. Encourage children to remember other books you have read together. What kinds of conflicts were developed?

When their discussion indicates that they understand what conflict in a plot means and they grasp the differences among the four broad types, ask children to use their learning logs for some further exploration in the books they are reading on their own. Organizing their comments in a chart like the one on page 27 (Figure 4) should be helpful.

Children could continue their exploration of conflict in other stories they read, extending a chart like the one above to facilitate comparisons.

Plot and Theme—What's the Difference?

Seeing the distinction between plot and theme is important in literary study. Without a sense of what a story is all about, we often read poorly; we don't know what to make of things. When children learn about theme, they can read more thoughtfully, making inferences about how a given character or event in the plot relates to the story as a whole.

The plot tells us what happens in a story: it is the sequence of events in which we learn about

From *Writing Journals*, published by GoodYearBooks. Copyright © 1996 Linda Western.

Figure 4

Title: *Julie of the Wolves*   Author: Jean Craighead George

Date read : _____

Conflict		Explanation
Person vs. Person	YES	The story opens as Julie flees from her arranged marriage.
Person vs. Nature	YES	The tundra is harsh, and Julie struggles to survive.
Person vs. Society	YES	Julie painfully experiences the changes to the Arctic brought by hunters in airplanes.
Person vs. Self	YES	Julie is torn: should she return to the tundra or go to her father, who may be one of the hunters?

the characters and the problems they face. In *Charlotte's Web*, for example, we learn how Wilbur the pig is saved from death, first by Fern and then by Charlotte. The theme, on the other hand, is the underlying idea that ties all of the elements of the story—plot, characters, setting—together. When we try to say, at the end of a story, what it was all about, or what its point is, we are grasping for a statement of the story's theme. In some stories, a single theme is evident; in others, there are several themes. We can say, for example, that *Charlotte's Web* is a story about true friendship, about the importance of interdependence, even about bravery; we could also say that it is an illustration of the cycle of life and death we all face.

Children can begin to understand how theme is developed through incidents in the plot by exploring the relationship graphically in webs like the one in Figure 5. Children can use their logs to create similar webs for the stories they are reading. What do they think the story is about? Their answers form the main headings on the web. What parts of the story led them to these conclusions? Their answers provide the information needed to complete the rest of the web.

NOTE: Teachers and children should remember that there is often a great deal of room for interpretation in identifying theme. A close look at *Charlotte's Web* certainly bears this out. Even the book's author, E. B. White, issues a caution: "I do hope, though, that you are not planning to turn *Charlotte's Web* into a moral tale. It is not that at all. It is, I think, an appreciative story, and there is quite a difference" (White, 1976, 613).

A Thematic Web of *Charlotte's Web*

Figure 5

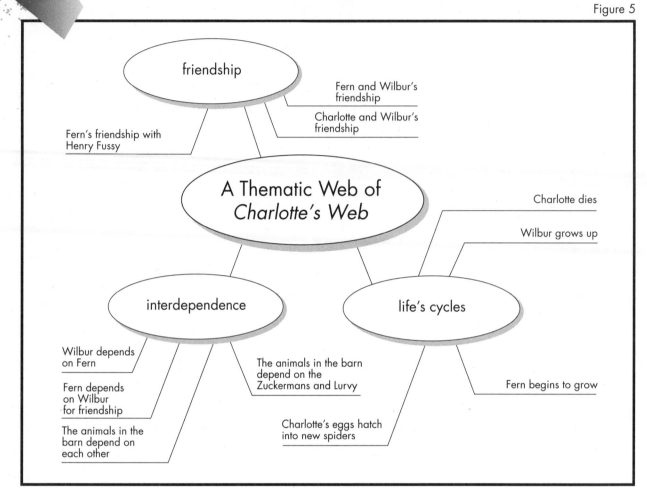

friendship

Fern and Wilbur's friendship

Charlotte and Wilbur's friendship

Fern's friendship with Henry Fussy

A Thematic Web of *Charlotte's Web*

Charlotte dies

Wilbur grows up

interdependence

life's cycles

Wilbur depends on Fern

Fern depends on Wilbur for friendship

The animals in the barn depend on each other

The animals in the barn depend on the Zuckermans and Lurvy

Charlotte's eggs hatch into new spiders

Fern begins to grow

From *Writing Journals*, published by GoodYearBooks. Copyright © 1996 Linda Western.

Figure 6

EXTENSION:

The pages of their logs offer a place to store children's thematic webs of other books. After they have created several, ask children to look at all of them together. Do any of the books develop similar themes? Children may want to create a chart like the one shown in Figure 6 to record the recurring themes they have discovered.

Friendship	Growth and Change
The Secret Garden	The Secret Garden
Charlotte's Web	Journey to Jo'Burg: A South African Story
Bridge to Terabithia	In the Year of the Boar and Jackie Robinson

Learning More About Authors and Illustrators

Children often like to learn more about favorite authors and illustrators. Some information is included on book jackets or is available from publishers. More extensive information can be found in sources like *Horn Book* and *The New Advocate* (both are periodicals). A whole series entitled *Something About the Author: Facts and Pictures about Contemporary Authors and Illustrators of Books for Young People* is available in many local libraries.

Since the latter sources are written for adults, you may want to read relevant material in them to the class. Before you read, ask children to make notes in their learning logs in response to the question: "What sort of person do you suppose the author of _____ must be?" After they have recorded their inferences, read selected passages and encourage the children to compare the new information with their earlier log entries. Taking the new information into account, they can elaborate on, or change, their inferences about the author. Then, as children read additional books by these authors and illustrators, they may begin by referring to their notes and speculating about how the writers' or artists' experiences may be reflected in the new story. These speculations, too, can be recorded in their logs.

For example, Cynthia Rylant grew up in Appalachia, where she lived with her grandparents and other relatives in a four-room house in Cool Ridge, Virginia. *When I Was Young in the Mountains* (1982) reflects that background of experiences. Do her other writings? Children could search through her other books to answer the question.

From *Writing Journals*, published by GoodYearBooks. Copyright © 1996 Linda Western.

Ask children to use their learning logs to make notes about books or poems they could write based on their own experiences. This could easily be the first step in a poem or story writing project.

Discovering Poetic Conventions

Learning logs can serve as a useful tool as children explore poetry. The following activity on similes and metaphors can be adapted to any set of experiences on other poetic elements, such as rhyme, repetition, rhythm; or poem types, such as narratives, haiku, concrete poetry (also known as shape poetry), and limericks.

Help children to see that similes and metaphors are really comparisons: "storm clouds are like galloping horses," "in dreaming, we open the mind's closets." We all use comparisons like these in our own speech to make sense of new things we see and hear. We try to understand things by comparing them to  what we already know. We often try to describe what is special about an event or experience by likening it to something else.

Poets do the same. But rather than teaching definitions, show children examples of comparisons at work in poems. Choose poems to read aloud that include many similes and metaphors—your search should be an easy one. Talk with children about what gets compared to what in each case. Ask children to use their learning logs to jot down those similes and metaphors that they find to be most interesting. Encourage them to use their logs to note additional examples as they read on their own. Then, ask them to use their notes in selecting a favorite poem to read to the class—a reading that should also include their explanation of why the similes and/or metaphors the poet uses are particularly appealing to them.

From *Writing Journals*, published by GoodYearBooks. Copyright © 1996 Linda Western.

Reader Response Journals

OBSERVATIONS AND INTERACTIONS

Making Predictions

Making predictions and then checking them against what really happens is an excellent approach for engaging children's interest in many learning activities. In this activity, children can use their reader response journals to make predictions about a book you are reading together in class. (This activity can also be adapted to reading children are doing on their own.) Journal pages should be divided into two columns: column 1 should be labeled **Predictions**; column 2, **What Happened.** After hearing or reading the first chapter, children will make their first prediction by answering the question, "What do I think will happen in the next chapter?" Their predictions should be recorded in column 1. After reading the second chapter, they will need to make two entries. In column 2, opposite their first prediction, they will summarize what actually happened. In column 1, they will write their prediction for the next chapter. The sharing of their entries should spark lively discussion both before and after each reading session.

EXTENSION:

Children can use some of the comparisons they have noted and/or use some of their own invention as they write their own new poem.

EXTENSION:

Children can use their entries to think further about the book. Do their entries show that the book was predictable? If so, did its predictability hold their attention or did it bore them? Perhaps instead they found the book to be surprising. If so, was it so surprising that the story was confusing or lacking in credibility?

What Sort of Place Is This? Settings That Create Moods

In many stories, the setting not only tells readers where and when a story takes place, but it also evokes a mood. For example, in *Little House in the Big Woods*, Laura Ingalls Wilder (1961) carefully paints word pictures of the warmth and coziness of the pioneers' cabin, contrasting it with the dangers outside. This contrast helps tell readers about the story, provided readers notice it. Noticing how an author uses setting to develop a story's mood can help all of us to read with insight.

Children can learn to recognize this aspect of an author's style. Here is one strategy involving the use of reader response journals. Ask children to place the name of the book they are reading (or one you are reading together in class) at the top of a page in their journals and draw a line down the middle of the page. In one column, ask them to write **Details of setting that are pleasant.** In the other, **Details of setting that are scary or sad.** Then, as they read, ask children to note their observations from the book in the appropriate column.

When they have done so, they should take stock of what they have found. What sort of setting is it? What mood does it suggest? Is that mood consistent with the plot?

EXTENSION:

Ask children to imagine that they are the author of the book they just read and have been asked by the book's publisher to write a letter of advice to the artist who will create a new set of illustrations. Their letters should advise the illustrator about the mood of the story and how it should be developed. Which scenes should be pictured? How should the characters' expressions be pictured? What colors should be used? Their journal entries should provide the information they will need in developing the plan.

Encourage children to share the early drafts of their letters in small groups so that others can offer critiques. An additional extension of the activity would be to commission a few artists from the class to produce illustrations, following the advice from the letters as closely as possible. A compilation of the final versions of the letters and illustrations will make a fascinating addition to your class library.

Noticing How Characters Change

In everyday life we sometimes hear exchanges of this sort: "How's your brother doing these days?" "Oh, fine; he hasn't changed a bit." Or we hear remarks of this sort: "I saw Jennifer yesterday. She's really changed." We look at people over time, and we notice changes.

Fictional characters often change, too, from when we first meet them to the final page. Anticipating these changes and noticing them when they do occur can help children gain new insights as they read. Reader response journals can facilitate this discovery.

Ask children to use their journals to create two webs for a main character in a book they are reading. The first should focus on what the character is like at the beginning of the story; the second should summarize what the character is like at the story's end. Since E. B. White's *Charlotte's Web* (1952) is such a familiar story, it serves as a useful example again here:

Figure 7

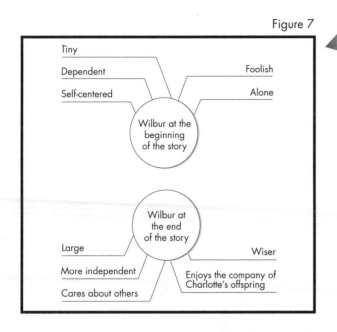

When their webs are completed, talk together about the results. Did children notice these changes while they were reading or only later? If a reader wanted to be sure to notice changes in a character as the story unfolds, what should the reader watch for? What are the signals that change is underway?

From *Writing Journals*, published by GoodYearBooks. Copyright © 1996 Linda Western.

EXTENSION:

Completed webs could be compiled into a collection called "Changing Characters" and added to your classroom library.

Children's exploration of character change can be extended further using a book you are reading together in class. After reading the first chapters—enough so that children have had a thorough introduction to the main character—pause and ask them to create a web that illustrates what they have learned about him/her so far. Then, ask them to make a second web that describes what they think the character will be like at the end of the story. Then read on to test their predictions.

As another extension, children can invent "Before and After" webs for a new character they would like to create a story about (see Figure 8). These webs can then be used as a resource when they actually begin writing.

What Would I Do in a Situation Like That?

When we hear about something that has happened to a friend or to somebody in the news, we often find ourselves speculating about what we would have done if we had been in that person's shoes. This journal activity encourages children to bring the same sort of speculative interest to the books they are reading.

Begin by asking children to divide one of their journal pages into two columns. The first column should be used to note each time the character has to make a decision. What choice must s/he make? Before reading further, children should use the second column to summarize the choice they themselves would make if they faced the same problem, under the same circumstances as those in the story.

As they read on, the children should begin to make comparisons. How do their choices compare to the character's? What benefits would follow from each choice? What disadvantages or costs would follow from each? Children can use their entries and the resulting comparisons in preparing a message of advice to the character. Their advice could be presented in any number of different ways—a friendly letter, a fax, a tape, a written warning—whatever format they think is most appropriate.

EXTENSION:

Children can refer to their entries in drawing a larger comparison between themselves and the character. In what ways are their personalities alike? different? What similarities and differences do they see in their goals? fears? aspirations? These comparisons could be presented in character sketches, character profiles, or graphically, in webs or charts.

Changing Characters

Figure 8

Name _____   Date _____

Book _____   Author _____

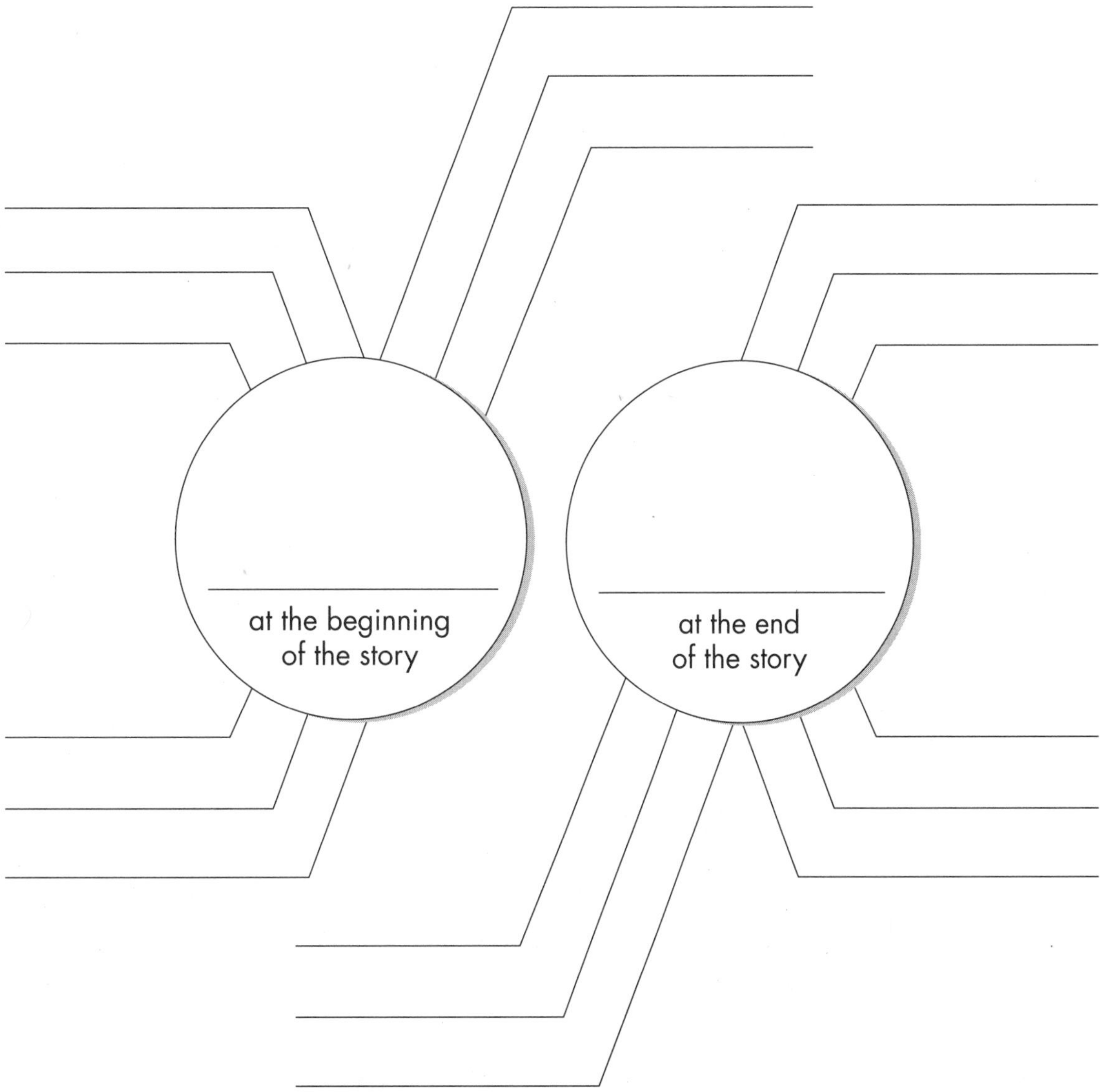

at the beginning
of the story

at the end
of the story

What Makes a Book Funny?

Children like funny books—we all do. In this reader response activity, children try to determine just what it is in a book that makes them laugh. Bring in a collection of humorous stories (some titles are listed under the subject heading "Wit and Humor" in *Subject Guide to Children's Books in Print*, which is updated annually). You might start with picture books. For example, in Ellen Raskin's *Nothing Ever Happens on My Block* (1989), the illustrations convey the humor. While the young narrator complains about his boring neighborhood, we see that he is completely oblivious to the chaotic events portrayed in the illustrations. In the books of Dr. Seuss (*If I Ran the Circus* [1956], for example), the comic illustrations combine with word play to create humor. On the other hand, there are many books where humor is developed primarily through characterizations and plot development in the text. Thomas Rockwell's *How to Eat Fried Worms* (1973) and Judy Blume's *Tales of a Fourth Grade Nothing* (1972) are long-standing favorites in books of this type.

After children have read a book that others (reviewers, book catalogers, teachers, or peers) have categorized as funny, ask them to use their journals to add their opinions. Do they agree? If so, what is it about the book that is amusing? If not, why not?

EXTENSION:

Working in pairs or small groups, children can switch books, make entries as they read, and then compare what they have written. Do they find that they are laughing at the same things or are there differences?

Clues in Illustrations

Illustrations provide an excellent avenue to explore in learning how an artist's use of line, shape, space, color, and texture can enhance a story's mood. Begin this activity by asking children to divide a page from their journals into two columns: label the first column **Illustrations** and the second **Text**. Then, have them page through a picture book they have chosen without reading, focusing instead on just the illustrations.

Children should use the first column to note what they learned from the illustrations. Where does the story take place? Who are the characters? Will this be a funny story, a frightening story, a story with a happy ending? Encourage them to include their reasons whenever possible. For example, do dark, somber colors suggest a frightening mood? Do smooth, flowing lines suggest a peaceful scene?

After they have made their notes, ask children to read the story. When they are done, they should use the second column to note what they learned from the text. Now compare the entries in the two columns. Do the illustrations complement the text? Does the overall mood of the illustrations match the story's mood? Do the illustrations add information to the text? Children's entries should provide many of the answers; these answers can then be used as the basis for a book talk.

NOTE: You may want to model this activity with the class before asking children to work independently. Many excellent books might help you get started, but consider these three: Trina Schart Hyman's illustrations in *Snow White* (1974), Jane Yolen's *Owl Moon* (1987), and Robert McCloskey's *Time of Wonder* (1957).

Ask children to add a third column to their journal pages. In this column they should write their suggestions for additional illustrations that might be added to the story to enhance the mood and illustrate the action. Encourage children to take another step and create what they have suggested.

What Kind of Mystery Do You Like? Creating a Survey

Many children in grades four to six will say that their favorite stories are mysteries. (There are many to choose from. *Subject Guide to Children's Books in Print* includes nearly 15 pages of titles!) But not all mysteries are alike, and readers are likely to differ in their preferences for the kind of mystery they especially like—something children will discover in this activity.

Begin by asking children to make a list in their journals of a few mysteries they have recently read or seen on television or at the movies. Ask them to add a brief description. Were they scary? adventurous? humorous? Was a crime or merely a kind of puzzle being solved? Were the characters predictable or surprising? Were the settings familiar or exotic?

Ask children to share their lists in small groups and talk about what they have written. How have they described the mysteries? Which kinds of mysteries do they prefer? Are their differences in the kinds of mysteries they like to read compared with those they like to watch?

Then have children look closely at the descriptions they have written. Can each group draw on them in developing a chart to use in surveying other children about their mystery preferences? What might they ask about the characters? the setting? the plot? The form in Figure 9 sets up some possible choices. For example, "Do you prefer mysteries that are scary or humorous?" "Do you like to be able to figure out the mystery or would you rather be surprised?" However, your

Mystery Preference Survey Form

Figure 9

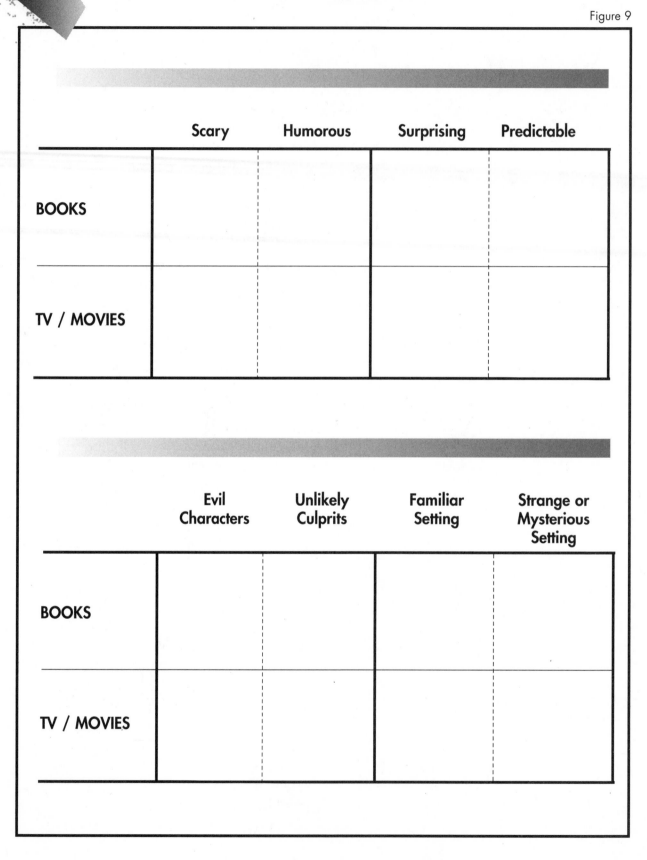

	Scary	Humorous	Surprising	Predictable
BOOKS				
TV / MOVIES				

	Evil Characters	Unlikely Culprits	Familiar Setting	Strange or Mysterious Setting
BOOKS				
TV / MOVIES				

From *Writing Journals*, published by GoodYearBooks. Copyright © 1996 Linda Western.

children may come up with a different approach. Each group should present its survey draft to the rest of the class. In discussion, decide together on a final form and ask everyone in the class to copy it into his/her journal.

Now it's time to conduct the survey. (Remind everyone to write down the names of the children they ask so there aren't duplicates.) When the surveys are complete, compile the findings. What preferences are revealed? Were there differences in preferences between the kinds of mysteries children like to read compared with those they like to watch?

From *Writing Journals*, published by GoodYearBooks. Copyright © 1996 Linda Western.

EXTENSION:

Children can conduct the same survey among adults and compare the results with the one conducted among children. Are there similarities? What are the differences?

This Story (Poem) Reminds Me Of…

Stories tell about people and events, real and imaginary. In a different way, however, stories tell us about other stories. Think about a cowboy movie, for example, in which two horsemen appear. One is young and handsome, and wears clothing that looks fresh and clean—even out on the dusty range. The other is older and grizzled, and wears a battered hat. What hunches do you have about these two? The young one is probably the hero; the older one is probably his sidekick. How do you know? Because you've seen this sort of duo before in other cowboy stories. The other stories, in effect, tell us about the new story.

That's how it is with many stories. Good readers know this; and, as they read a new story, they keep in mind patterns and archetypes from other stories they have read. Those stories help them understand what they're reading now.

This activity is designed to lead children to draw parallels between the books they are reading and other poems or stories they have already read or heard. As they read, ask them to note whether and how the characters remind them of others. Are there similarities in personalities? in the problems that are faced? in the settings? in the theme? in the writers' styles?

Children's entries should be made as they read through a book rather than when they've finished. Entries should be dated so that children can see how their opinions change over time. Similarities that seemed obvious in the first chapters may disappear and new ones may emerge in subsequent chapters.

EXTENSION:

This activity could also take the opposite approach: children could use the phrase "This story (poem) is different from anything I have ever read before because … " as a basis for their entries. As indicated above, entries should be made as they are reading.

Which Version Do I Like Best?

Making comparisons can help children learn how to talk about literature and to express their literary preferences. Because they are so accessible, folk tales and Mother Goose rhymes provide ideal material for comparison activity, though this strategy can easily be adapted to other reading (for example, biographies about the same subject, or two books by the same author or illustrator).

Help children to find at least two versions of the same folk tale or browse through two

Version Preference Form

Figure 10

VERSION A — I like:

VERSION A — I don't like:

VERSION B — I like:

VERSION B — I don't like:

Based on what I have written above, I prefer _____

_____

_____

_____

different Mother Goose collections with them. (Most local libraries have several different editions of familiar stories from the Brothers Grimm, for example, and there should be a number of collections of nursery rhymes to choose from.) Ask children to divide a page from their reader response journals into four boxes and label them as shown in Figure 10. Then, as they read, children should fill in the boxes. What did they like about each version? What did they dislike? Based on their entries in each box, which version do they prefer? Children can then present both versions to others in the class and use the material from their journal as the basis for explaining why they prefer one version over the other.

From *Writing Journals*, published by GoodYearBooks. Copyright © 1996 Linda Western.

EXTENSION:

Children can repeat the activity above, only this time ask them to imagine that they are a child in kindergarten. Their preferences should be made from the point of view of a five-year-old! Then encourage them actually to read the two stories to younger children in order to test their hypotheses.

Tell It to the Judge

Introduce children to the two most well-known awards in children's literature: the Caldecott Medal and the Newbery Medal, both awarded annually by a committee of the Association for Library Services for Children of the American Library Association (ALA). The winners of these annual awards, as well as the runners-up, are easy to spot because replicas of the medals appear on the books' covers. You will also find listings of winners and honors books in many sources, including *Children's Books in Print.*

Ask children to select one of the award winners or honor books and use their journals to respond to the statement, "I agree (disagree) with the judges that this book should be a medal winner because…" Tell children that they will use their entries as the basis for a "book talk" that they will be giving to their class. In their talks, they will be asked to comment on why they agree or disagree, and to speculate on why they think a panel of adult judges awarded the prize.

EXTENSION:

Invite your school and community librarian into your classroom to hear the children's presentations. Ask the librarian to tell your students about other prizes awarded in children's literature.

Remembering Special Poems

Encourage children to keep an ongoing log of poems they have especially enjoyed and the sources where they can be found. Norton (1992) suggests that the log can be organized by topic (nature, holidays, feelings, etc.) or according to its expression of a particular poetic element such as rhythm, rhyme, or imagery. In addition to title, poet, and source, children should add a comment about why they find the poem to be particularly enjoyable. The log format might look something like the one shown in Figure 11.

EXTENSION:

Children can establish a class file of poetry favorites. The file can be kept in a three-ring notebook or filed, by heading, on cards.

Figure 11

Topic or Element	Poem	Poet	Source	Comment

From *Writing Journals*, published by GoodYearBooks. Copyright © 1996 Linda Western.

Discovering Personal Reading Preferences

Give each of your students a copy of the chart found on page 41 (Figure 12) for inclusion in their reader response journals. Ask children to print the title of each book they read and the date they finished reading it in the vertical rows. They should put check marks in the appropriate horizontal rows to indicate what they see as each story's significant attributes. The chart also provides a place where they can record their summary evaluations. Over time, this chart will provide a graphic summary of the books the children have read, and it will help them to discover patterns in their reading interests.

EXTENSION:

Children may wish to create their own versions of this chart by substituting the attributes in the example with those they name themselves. In another variation, genre names can be substituted for attributes.

Reading Log

Figure 12

Name _____

TITLE:

Funny									
Happy									
Exciting									
Adventurous									
Scary									
Mysterious									
Fact-filled									
Sad									
Troubling									
Predictable									

OPINIONS:

A favorite									
Didn't want to finish									
Boring									
Couldn't put it down									

OBSERVATIONS AND INTERACTIONS

Consider the Source:
Exploring Point of View

The author's choice of a narrator can profoundly affect the way a story unfolds. What and how much we learn about the other characters and the plot depends on who tells the story—one of the characters or an omniscient narrator. Good readers know this, and it affects their reading. They notice who is telling the story and, if it is a character, what it is about him/her that might have an impact on how the story is told.

This writer's notebook activity helps children to see these differences for themselves. While this activity can be easily adapted for use with many kinds of books, let's begin with the wordless picture book *Frog Goes to Dinner,* by Mercer Mayer (1977), as an example. In pictures only, we "read" the story of how a frog  slips into a boy's pocket just as the boy and his family leave for a dinner out. The frog's appearance at the family's table in the restaurant leads to hilarious if not disastrous results.

Ask children to rewrite this brief story in two ways: they can choose to tell it from the point of view of the frog, the boy, his sister, the boy's mother, the boy's father, the waiter at the restaurant, or someone else at the restaurant—or they can invent a narrator who knows everything about each of the characters and the plot itself. For example, what would the frog say about his misadventures? Why did he hop into the boy's pocket? Did he mean to hop into the lady's salad? What would the boy say?

Would he start his story at the restaurant or would he begin by telling about other mischief the frog had gotten into before this incident? How would the mother tell her story? Did she think what happened was funny or is she still angry? Could she know why the frog hopped into the pocket?

Encourage children to have others read and critique their early drafts. When the story is told from a character's point of view, for example, is anything stated that that character couldn't know about?

After the children have done their rewriting, ask them to read their new stories. How do their two versions differ? How are they alike? How do they compare with the stories of other children who have chosen different points of view?

EXTENSION:

Children can continue to experiment with point of view in several ways: by continuing the exercise illustrated above with another wordless picture book, by rewriting an incident from a book they are reading using a different narrator, or by creating a new piece of writing, trying it from several narrative points of view in order to decide which is most effective.

A Penny for Your Thoughts:
Writing a Character's Diary

Some stories tell the reader a great deal about what the characters are thinking. Even in these stories, however, there may be interesting gaps—points in the story where we know a given character must be having thoughts, but isn't sharing them. These undisclosed thoughts amount to an untold story—a story waiting to be brought out.

In this journal activity, children gain new insights into a character and also gather experience in writing from a new perspective. First, they imagine themselves as a character in the story they are reading, and that this character keeps a diary. Then, as they read, they make diary entries in their writers' notebooks from the point of view of that character. (They should make frequent entries, writing only about the material they have just read.) Encourage children to write about how the character is responding to what is happening to him/her now and what s/he might be anticipating. They will also have to remember to write in the way they imagine the character would.

From *Writing Journals*, published by GoodYearBooks. Copyright © 1996 Linda Western.

EXTENSION:

Have a tape recorder available so that children can read and record their entries. Encourage them to listen to what they have recorded and to make changes in their notebooks whenever they see ways to make what they have written sound more like the character. Once children are satisfied, the recordings should be made available for others to hear.

Advice to an Author

As children read, ask them to write entries in their writers' notebooks about what they like and don't like about the books they are reading. Are the characters credible? Is there enough action to keep the plot moving? Does the author tell the story in an interesting way?

Children should use these entries as they prepare a letter to the author in which they offer advice for his/her next book. What should the author write about? Who might the characters be? What

should the author continue to do? What should s/he improve upon?

EXTENSION:

Establish a three-ring binder in your classroom library for a final copy of children's letters. Next to each letter, place a blank piece of paper for the comments of other children who have read books by the same author. On this sheet, children can write whether they agree or disagree with the writer of the letter, and why.

Let Me Tell You Why We Say That!

Like the tales and myths of folklore, many familiar expressions have been passed down to us from generation to generation through the oral tradition. (See **Developing an Understanding of Folklore and the Oral Tradition**, pages 21–22.) We use these expressions in our daily speech; authors often have their characters use them, too. For example, we hear, read, or may even say things like: "It's raining cats and dogs," "A bird in the hand is worth two in the bush," "He's way out on a limb," or "They're a bunch of unhappy campers." In each case, we infer the meaning of the expression—it can't be taken literally.

During a brainstorming session in class, make a list together of expressions like these. Children should then spend several days listening for other examples as they hear people speaking at school, in their neighborhoods, on television and on the radio, recording what they hear in their writers' notebooks.

During a class session, ask everyone to share the expressions they have discovered and complete the master list. As a next step, ask everyone to select one expression from the list and create a story in their notebooks explaining when and how it was first said. Working in groups, children should read each others' drafts and critique them.

Does the story provide a satisfactory explanation? What could be clarified? Have children use their notebooks to rework their drafts until they are satisfied. Their finalized stories can be collected into a class book and placed in either the classroom or school library.

EXTENSION:

Schedule a story reading session so that the writers can share their stories. The audience could be another class, children's parents, residents in a retirement center, or another group in your community. (Some children may want to illustrate their stories.)

Writing A Character Biography

From time to time we see someone—on a bus, at the grocery store, in a crowd—who catches our attention. We wonder about this person's story. Who is s/he? What experiences has s/he had? This activity builds on the same sort of curiosity about a fictional character who has a story waiting to be told.

Lead up to this activity by asking children to keep a special section in their writers' notebooks to record notes about interesting characters they meet as they read. Their entries may be about the characters themselves or about the problems they face. Children should also note the techniques authors use to help readers get to know these characters (see **Getting to Know You, Getting to Know All About You: Character Development in Fiction**, page 23).

Eventually children will use their entries to select a book character who could be an intriguing subject for a biography. Their entries also should be helpful as they look for ways to tell about their character. And, they can use their writers' notebooks as they plan out what ques-

tions the biography should answer. (For example, "What experiences did the character have before readers meet him/her?" "What happened to that character after the final chapter?")

EXTENSION:

Character biographies can be collected into an anthology for your classroom library.

Writing Poetry

"Encourage children to read and write poetry and they will be encouraged to reach into themselves and articulate feelings and dreams." These are among the introductory remarks found in Karla Kuskin's *Near the Window Tree: Poems and Notes* (1975, 5), an unusual book that provides an ideal resource for showing chil-

dren how notebook entries can inspire poetry writing. On the left-hand page of double-page spreads, we read Kuskin's notes revealing where she got the idea for the poem that appears on the right-hand page. (In some cases, an idea leads to more than one poem.)

Present this book to children and provide time for them to explore it themselves. Point out how Kuskin's poems are inspired by moods, memories, sounds, and sights. Encourage children to do just what Kuskin has done by storing their own interesting thoughts and ideas in their writers' notebooks. Eventually they can build a poem around one that seems particularly interesting. Allot enough time to this project so that children have plenty of opportunities to look around them for ideas. Their writers' notebooks should serve as storehouses here—for collecting ideas and later for working through them.

From *Writing Journals*, published by GoodYearBooks. Copyright © 1996 Linda Western.

In her introduction, Kuskin explains her concern for the formality that often marks the way children are introduced to poetry. "The very young have an easy affinity for rhythm and the sounds of words. This can be smothered by emphasizing complex rules and unfamiliar subject matter instead of stressing familiar speech and humor, the simplicity and lyric quality of so much verse" (Kuskin, 1975, 6).

However, Myra Cohn Livingston avoids the formality and obscurity found all too often in resources about poetry. In Poem-Making: Ways to Begin Writing Poetry *(1991) she uses a direct and informal style, peppered with easy to understand examples, to help children hear the voices of poetry—lyrical, narrative, and dramatic. She also includes sections on sound and rhyme as well as other poetic elements: repetition, alliteration, and assonance, for example. There is a section on simile, metaphor, and personification, and a final section on other forms of poetry: haiku, cinquain, limericks, free verse, and concrete (shape) poetry. Each section includes suggestions for how children might incorporate what they have just learned about into their own poetry. Introduce children to this resource and encourage them to try out some of Livingston's suggestions.*

Creating a Fanciful Character

Go with children to the picture book section of your school or local library. As they browse, ask children to use their notebooks to comment on the fanciful characters they find in so many books, the kinds of characters they see and read about that couldn't exist in real life: animals that live like people, friendly and scary monsters, and so on. Children should be sure to comment on which of these characters seem particularly fun to read about and why.

Then ask children to use their notes in creating a fantastic character of their own. They should describe their character's physical appearance, its personality, and what it is that makes him/her/it a candidate for fantasy. Encourage children to read their description to others and make any necessary changes in order to make the description complete. Their notebook would be an excellent place for sketches of the character, too.

There are so many possibilities here. It may be enough for children to tell others about their character, or to write a brief character sketch. On the other hand, this may be the perfect launching point for creating a story built around the imaginary character.

Writing an Original Myth

Long a classroom favorite, this activity also lends itself to writers' notebooks. Before beginning, children should have had many experiences listening to and reading myths. (You can find many examples, bound individually or in collections, in the folk literature section of your library.) Encourage children to make notes, perhaps lists, about these myths as they learn about them. What do the myths explain? Where were they first told? What sorts of problems must be resolved? How are the problems solved? Are they solved through the cunning of the characters, through good luck, or because of the intervention of a god of goddess? Notebook entries can serve as a launching point for an original myth as children plan their own versions of existing myths or create completely new ones.

From *Writing Journals*, published by GoodYearBooks. Copyright © 1996 Linda Western.

EXTENSION:

Using the notes and drafts from their writers' notebooks, children can write a final version of their myths. Perhaps they will want to present it as an original book with illustrations.

 Planning a Sequel

We leave many stories wishing there were more to read. We want to know more about the characters and what might happen to them after the events on the last page. This activity builds on that kind of interest and also helps children to understand how stories are structured.

Begin by having children divide a page from their writers' notebooks into two columns, adding headings to both like those in the example (Figure 13). The first column should be reserved for their notes on a book they are reading. The second column will be used for planning that story's sequel.

Have children use their notes as the basis for an oral report in which they tell others about the stories they have read and the plans they have made for a book that could follow.

EXTENSION:

A logical extension, of course, is to write either a portion of the planned sequel (the first or last chapter, for example) or the entire book if children's interest is sufficient.

Changing Genres—Poetry to Prose (and vice versa!)

Some children are bothered by the format of poetry. Because poems often look different from other reading material, children reason, they must be very complicated and hard to understand. This activity is designed to take the mystery out of poetry by helping children to discover that poems often tell stories or describe ideas, just as other kinds of writing do.

Begin by sharing lots of poetry with children. You won't have any trouble finding selections. *Subject Guide to Children's Books in Print* lists pages of titles to choose from, including some arranged by topic: nature, animals, humorous, etc. Once children have had many experiences in reading and hearing poetry, ask them to select a particular favorite and copy it into their writers' notebooks. Then, ask them to try rewriting that poem into a descriptive paragraph or perhaps even a story. Encourage children to ask others in the class to read both the poem and their initial drafts. Remind them that they may want to consider incorporating their classmates' suggestions into subsequent drafts.

Once they are satisfied with what they have written, ask children to copy both the original poem and the prose version onto pages that will be included in a classroom poetry/prose anthology. Have them prepare an accompanying tape for each poetry/prose pair. Let

Planning a Sequel

Figure 13

Name _____ Date _____

Title:

_____

When and where the story takes place:

_____
_____
_____
_____

Main characters:

_____
_____
_____
_____

Main events:

_____
_____
_____
_____
_____
_____

Conclusion:

_____
_____
_____

Sequel:

_____

When and where the story takes place:

_____
_____
_____
_____

Main characters:

_____
_____
_____
_____

Main events:

_____
_____
_____
_____
_____
_____

Conclusion:

_____
_____
_____

them discover for themselves the differences in how poetry and prose sound!

As the title of this activity suggests, this activity can be reversed. Any part of a story could be turned into a poem—free verse or rhyming.

Jokes, Riddles, and Word Play

Children often enjoy poring over the many joke and riddle books that are available (see the sections labeled "Wit and Humor" and "Riddles" in *Subject Guide to Children's Books in Print* for scores of possible titles). In this writing activity they can try their hands at creating jokes of their own.

Begin by reminding children that their writers' notebooks are ideal places for recording favorite jokes as well as words and word combinations that strike them as funny—possibly even ideas for funny characters and/or plots. This section of their notebooks can be a storage bin to delve into from time to time. Is there material here for a new joke or riddle? Children can adapt existing jokes or create entirely new ones based on something they have recorded. Remind everyone to try out their new jokes on others in their class. Are revisions needed after the first telling? Their notebooks can be used to develop new drafts until the jokes are in their final form.

Encourage children to enter their jokes into a class joke book, which is part of the class library. Some may want to add illustrations.

Play Making

In this notebook activity, children adapt a favorite scene from a story into a play format. In doing so, they should gain important insights into what the audience needs to know about the whole story in order to understand the scene. They also will need to determine how much of the new play will be told by the narrator and how much can be carried by dialogue.

Begin by asking children to be on the lookout for chapters or scenes in the stories they read that would lend themselves to the stage, noting the possibilities in their notebooks. Remind them that their decisions should be based not only on the potential the scene has for capturing the audience's interest, but also on practicality. Can the scene be successfully staged without elaborate props?

Once they have selected what that scene should be, have them use their writers' notebooks to turn that scene into a script. They will need to draft dialogue and any explanatory comments from the narrator. Encourage them to try out what they have written on other listeners. Can they follow the story? What has to be added? changed? Corrections should be made in their notebooks until a final draft is decided upon.

Plan a special theater program for other classes in your school in which children actually perform what they have written. They may want to select music as an introduction, background, and/or conclusion that enhances the mood they are trying to create.

From *Writing Journals*, published by GoodYearBooks. Copyright © 1996 Linda Western.

References

CHILDREN'S BOOKS REFERRED TO IN THIS SECTION

Burnett, F. H. 1987. *The Secret Garden.* (T. Tudor, Illus.) New York: HarperCollins

Blume, J. (1972). *Tales of a Fourth-Grade Nothing.* (R. Doty, Illus.) New York: Dutton.

Chase, R. (1943). *The Jack Tales.* (B. Williams, Jr., Illus.) New York: Houghton Mifflin.

Fitzhugh, L. (1964). *Harriet the Spy.* New York: HarperCollins.

George, J. (1974). *Julie of the Wolves.* (J. Schoenherr, Illus.) New York: HarperCollins.

Grimm, J. and Grimm, W. K. (1979). *Snow White.* (T. S. Hyman, Illus.) New York: Little, Brown & Co.

Kuskin, K. (1975) *Near the Window Tree: Poems and Notes.* New York: HarperCollins.

Livingston, M. C. (1991). *Poem-Making: Ways to Begin Writing Poetry.* New York: HarperCollins.

MacLachlan, P. (1980). *Arthur for the Very First Time.* (L. Bloom, Illus.) New York: HarperCollins.

Mayer, M. (1974). *Frog Goes to Dinner.* New York: Dial.

McCloskey, R. (1957). *Time of Wonder.* New York: Viking.

Naidoo, B. (1986). *Journey to Jo'burg: A South African Story.* (E. Velasquez, Illus.) New York: HarperCollins.

Paterson, K. (1977). *Bridge to Terabithia.* (D. Diamond, Illus.) New York: HarperCollins.

Raskin, E. (1989). *Nothing Ever Happens on My Block.* New York: Macmillan.

Rockwell, T. (1973). *How to Eat Fried Worms.* (E. McCully, Illus.) New York: Watts.

Rodgers, M. (1972). *Freaky Friday.* New York: HarperCollins.

Ruckman, I. (1984). *Night of the Twisters.* New York: HarperCollins.

Rylant, C. (1985). *When I Was Young in the Mountains.* New York: Dutton.

Seuss, Dr. (1956). *If I Ran the Circus.* New York: Random Books for Young Readers.

Sierra, J. (1992). *The Oryx Multicultural Folktale Series.* (J. Caroselli, Illus.) Phoenix, AZ: The Oryx Press.

Soto, Gary. (1993). *Local News.* New York: Harcourt, Brace Jovanovich.

White, E. B. (1952). *Charlotte's Web.* (G. Williams, Illus.) New York: HarperCollins.

Wilder, L. I. (1961). *Little House in the Big Woods.* Rev. ed. (G. Williams, Illus.) New York: HarperCollins.

Yolen, J. (1992). *Street Rhymes Around the World.* (Illus. by 17 international artists) Honesdale, PA: Boyds Mills Press, Inc.

Yolen, J. (1987). *Owl Moon.* (J. Schoenherr, Illus.) New York: Putnam.

BIBLIOGRAPHY OF SOURCES ON BOOK MAKING

Following is a partial list of resources from which you and your class can gather information on how books are planned and published.

Aliki. (1986). *How a Book is Made.* New York: Thomas Y. Crowell.

Tracing the evolution of a commercially published book from the completion of the manuscript, to its editing, printing, review, and promotion, Aliki has supplemented her own text with illustrations in cartoon format. Particular attention is paid to the color separation and printing processes.

Goldenberg, C. (1993). "The Design and Typography of Children's Books." *The Horn Book.* September/October, 559-567

This article describes the role of the book designer in the publication of a book. The author includes a discussion of typography, the relationship of text to paper, practical considerations (such as how long the book can be), and the reasons why a book jacket must be eye-catching. Goldenberg also offers a chronological account of the steps in turning a manuscript into a finished book. All of this information is well within the middle grade child's ability to understand.

Purdy, S. (1973). *Books for You to Make*. Philadelphia: J. B. Lippincott Company.

The emphasis here is on transforming a manuscript into a bound book. This is a "how to" book: how to prepare a dummy; how to decide upon a design, layout, and illustrations; and how to bind a book (several techniques are described). A final section describes how text and artwork are printed in commercially published books. Because of technological changes in the years since this book was published, some of the content in the last section is now somewhat dated, but the balance is still relevant and helpful to middle graders who would like to make their own books.

Weiss, H. (1974). *How to Make Your Own Books*. New York: Thomas Y. Crowell Company

Step-by-step directions, enhanced by illustrations, help readers to create a variety of books—not only those with conventional bindings, but Japanese-style books, scrolls, pop-ups, and books in unique shapes. There are suggestions for finding cover materials (including directions for making marbleized paper), as well as ideas for types of books to make: travel journals, diaries, flip books, photo and stamp albums, comic and nonsense books, and experimental books. This book is well suited to readers in grades four to six.

Journal Writing and Social Studies

From *Writing Journals*, published by GoodYearBooks. Copyright © 1996 Linda Western.

An Overview

Learning Logs

OBSERVATIONS AND INTERACTIONS

The Learning Log and the Daily Lesson
The Learning Log and the Field Trip
The Learning Log and the Textbook
Making Connections: Life Then and Now

EXPLORATION AND RESEARCH

A Window on the Working World
What's Really in the Comics?
A Unique Summary: Creating a Political Cartoon
Tying It All Together: Making a Geographic Web
What Music Can Tell Us About History
Developing an Inquiry Chart

Reader Response Journals

OBSERVATIONS AND INTERACTIONS

Understanding Consequences
Illustrations Tell a Story, Too
Facts in Fiction
Biography and History—An Important Partnership

EXPLORATION AND RESEARCH

Little Things Mean a Lot: Studying Folk Tale Variants
Exploring Cultures through Their Tales: Tricksters Around the World
Discovering the World of Mythology
Looking at Biographies and Autobiographies with a Critic's Eye

Writers' Notebooks

OBSERVATIONS AND INTERACTIONS

What's Happening? A Personal Outlook on a Current Event
A Fresh Look at Familiar Places: Looking at Your State (Community) as a Tourist
Learning Through Personal History
Expanding Meanings Through Poetry

EXPLORATION AND RESEARCH

Applying RAFT
Creating a Conversation
An Eyewitness to History: Writing a Biographical Sketch
Working as Historians Do

References

A Sampling of Trickster Tales
A Sampling of Folk Tale Variants
A Sampling of Myths Explaining the Seasons
Other Children's Books Referred to in This Section

Overview

Elementary social studies is typically interdisciplinary. Though history and geography are emphasized, the work children do in this general subject area can include study in anthropology, economics, political science (or civics), and sociology. But while the combinations of disciplines are likely to vary from unit to unit, maybe even from day to day, the objectives for study that social studies educators recommend are strikingly similar. "Students must use creative and critical thinking skills for problem-solving, decision-making, and resolving differences. Students must also develop and use strategies that help them to be independent learners and responsible citizens. They must learn to work together with their peers through cooperative and collaborative efforts" (Farris & Cooper, 1994, 15).

Journal-writing activities can help teachers to meet these objectives. As children engage in acts of observing, describing, explaining, and imagining, their journal entries provide an on-going record of their thoughts, preserving them for subsequent elaboration and new uses. For example:

■ Writing helps children gain a better understanding of the ideas they study. When children write about a topic before they read about it, their writing activates their prior knowledge and helps them make sense of what they read. When they write as they read, or after reading, their writing helps them keep track of what they have noticed and aids them in fitting their observations into a larger pattern of understanding. Journals—whether they are learning logs, literature response journals, writers' notebooks, or dialogue journals—provide ideal places for children to work as they record their thinking.

■ Well-chosen prompts for journal writing help children to make connections between their own worlds and the topics under study, which at first glance might seem very remote to them.

■ Children maintain their interest in social studies when they write in a variety of forms about social studies topics (Walley, 1991). Journals offer opportunities for children to write in many different styles: persuasive, expository, narrative, and even in poetic language.

■ Report writing, the staple of so much schoolwork, is justifiably criticized when it means merely that children research an assigned topic by paraphrasing what encyclopedias have to say about it. James Moffett and Betty Jane Wagner sum up these criticisms: "… educators think…that students are being taught to do scholarly research when they're in fact just summarizing summaries" (1992, 386). Journal-writing activities can lead children away from this sterile, formulaic approach. In journals, children can formulate problems, ask questions, record observations, compare examples with counter-examples, and propose interpretations. In other words, journals help children carry out real research.

■ Children can use their journal entries to practice using symbols, pictures, graphs, tables, maps, and timelines. Graphic figuration in these forms and others helps children to organize information and to give form to their thoughts.

■ Social studies educators strongly endorse the use of literature in the social studies curriculum. Well-written historical fiction provides young readers with a window into lives and times of the past. Stories of other cultures and unfamiliar places, whether the setting is contemporary or historical, can greatly extend children's understanding. Children's use of literature response journals enhances these educational experiences. "Written response to literature is a powerful means of preserving those special transactions with books that make reading a rewarding, personal journey" (Hancock, 1993, 467).

■ Journal entries can help to enliven and extend textbook-oriented instruction. Children gain a better grasp of concepts if they spend time writing in journals or logs about what they have read in their social studies texts (Kuhrt, 1989).

Because the scope of elementary social studies is broad, *Writing Journals* presents a wide range of suggested activities. Some can be adapted to any social studies field; others are more specific. The sources suggested for children to use are similarly varied: textbooks, fiction, nonfiction, conversations, newspapers, maps, television, radio, and even cartoons.

Use these suggestions as springboards for your own ideas. Adapt them freely to fit your students, your curriculum, and your own teaching interests and specialties.

Learning Logs

OBSERVATIONS AND INTERACTIONS

The Learning Log and the Daily Lesson

Whenever appropriate, begin a class session with a five-minute writing activity prompted by a question directly related to the objective for that day's instruction. For example:

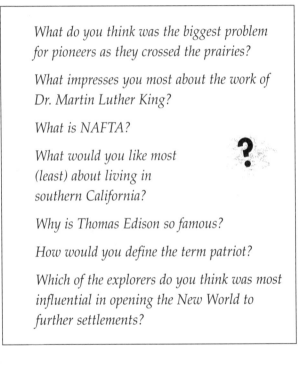

What do you think was the biggest problem for pioneers as they crossed the prairies?

What impresses you most about the work of Dr. Martin Luther King?

What is NAFTA?

What would you like most (least) about living in southern California?

Why is Thomas Edison so famous?

How would you define the term patriot?

Which of the explorers do you think was most influential in opening the New World to further settlements?

Two reasons for this activity are particularly compelling. First, it establishes a focus and sets a tone for the class time to follow. Engaging children immediately in thoughtful work is invigorating and paves the way for further purposeful work. Children's early journal entries also provide them with something to say in subsequent discussion—something to react to and against as they continue to read, discuss, listen, and watch.

Whenever possible, conclude the class with another five-minute writing session in which children summarize what they have learned. They may also go beyond summaries, making conjectures and raising questions to guide further study.

From *Writing Journals*, published by GoodYearBooks. Copyright © 1996 Linda Western.

EXTENSION:

Children's log entries in the activity described above have an immediate application in the classroom. For further applications, encourage children to look over their entries on their own. Which questions warrant further study? What is still unclear? Review of this sort helps children to move forward to further research. It also provides them with a self-portrait of themselves as learners. How much did they know before beginning a unit? What did they learn? Are they satisfied with what and how they have learned?

The Learning Log and the Field Trip

Many teachers work hard to plan and carry out field trips. And, many teachers are deeply disappointed at the results: children getting bored and restless in the museum, for example, or paying no attention during the guided tour of the courthouse. What can be done to minimize these unhappy results? Successful teachers emphasize preparation and reflection. They make the outing itself a part of a larger project, one that begins and ends in an effort to learn something new.

One way to help children see these connections is through journal writing. Introduce the trip by asking children to list all of the things they already know about where they are going on a page from their learning logs. (Remind them to leave plenty of space between items on their list.) Then, ask them to make a another list, on a second page, of what they would like to learn.

Children should take their logs along on the day of the trip. Encourage them to record observations and write responses to the questions they have asked. They should also add to and/or revise the first section of their log entries. Has the field trip caused them to change their minds? Did something they thought they knew prove to be incorrect? Did the visit help them to elaborate on what they already knew?

When you return, children's log entries should serve as the basis for linking the field trip to the ongoing project of which it is a part. They may be used to plan a debate, to structure a simulation, to provide a focus for a story, and so on.

EXTENSION:

Ask children to use their logs to list questions that were prompted by the trip. Did they discover something new that they would like to find out about? Do they want to check other sources in order to learn more or to verify the accuracy of something they saw or read about? Children can use these entries as the basis for further research, either as a part of a school assignment or in order to follow up on their own interests.

NOTE: This activity can be adapted to any sort of field trip in study throughout grades four to six.

The Learning Log and the Textbook

Because research has shown that children learn more from their textbooks when they write about what they have read there (Kuhrt, 1989), this learning log activity may be particularly useful. Before children begin reading a textbook assignment, establish a purpose for the reading—an intellectual purpose ("we're going to try to find out why so many people moved from small towns into cities in the 1920s"), not a procedural one ("you're going to be tested on this"). Remind children to read with this purpose in mind, noticing ideas and information related to the question(s) it raises.

After finishing the assigned pages, ask children to close their textbooks, open their logs and list everything they can remember that bears on the set purpose. (By writing with their books closed, children will need to use their own words.) Then, working in small groups, ask children to share what they have written. As a group, their task is to agree upon what should be included in a master list. As they work, encourage children to talk together about their choices. How often do students note the same information? What might account for some of the differences?

Ask students to add the agreed-upon list to their logs. Remind them that these lists can be very helpful when studying for a test, developing a report, etc.

From *Writing Journals*, published by GoodYearBooks. Copyright © 1996 Linda Western.

EXTENSION:

The master list of each group can become the basis of a class discussion or a more ambitious project. In either case, use the entries, as they have been refined by discussion, to answer the question(s) posed at the outset. The answer, of course, may be incomplete or contested, depending upon the adequacy of the information provided in the textbook.

NOTE: This learning log activity can be applied to any unit, and in fact to any subject area. It also can be adapted to study after students have seen a movie or videotape in class.

Making Connections: Life Then and Now

Social studies educators emphasize the importance of social history—the history of everyday life. The following learning log activity is designed with this dimension of history in mind. Begin by asking children to divide a page

from their learning logs into two columns. The first should be headed **Life Now**, the second, **Life Then**. Ask children to place the following subheadings at intervals within each column: **Environment, Needs, Recreation, Difficulties.** Have them fill in the left-hand column based on their own day-to-day experiences as fourth-, fifth-, or sixth-graders.

Then, as you introduce a new historical unit, ask children to imagine how someone exactly their age, living at the time being studied, would respond to the same prompts. Tell them that, as they read textbooks, other nonfiction sources, and historical fiction, and as they see videos and movies related to the topic at hand, they should fill in the second column based on information those sources present and on what that information leads them to believe.

Next, children can make some comparisons. How similar are the entries in the two columns? What are the differences? This completed log page should provide children with insights and bases for meaningful discussion.

EXTENSION:

Ask children to use their entries to prepare a character sketch written in first person. They should name the character whose answers they imagined in their learning log (I am _____); the first paragraph they write should describe that person. In subsequent paragraphs, the fictional character should explain what his or her life is like. Children can use the entries in each of the subheadings as the basis for a new paragraph. The completed sketches can be presented to others in the class, either orally or in writing.

This activity is especially likely to work well if you can also devise a plausible occasion and audience for the final version of the completed sketch. There are many possibilities. For example, perhaps the character is writing home to her family, to tell how her life has evolved in her new home. Or perhaps (with a shift to third-person) the sketch can be converted to a newspaper obituary.

EXPLORATION AND RESEARCH

A Window on the Working World

This activity, a variation of a class field trip, would fit well into a unit on government and/or economics. After making the necessary appointments and other arrangements, children should set off on this trip (which can be to a business, a state or municipal office, or even a farm) with a set of predetermined questions, which they have entered in their logs. Some examples might be:

What work is done here?

How is that work accomplished?

Who is employed?

How did they get their jobs?

Who are the customers?

What is the importance of this work to others?

There should be time during the trip for children simply to watch what is going on and to summarize what they see in their logs. There should be time, too, for questions. If possible, questions should be addressed to several people in addition to the tour guide. Children should also collect brochures and pamphlets to study later.

Rather than entering into a class discussion when you return, involve children immediately in the task of developing their own responses to

the place they have visited, based on their log entries and their reactions to the printed material. And, instead of writing reports, ask them to summarize their responses in a different format: a want ad the company might place that not only describes a particular position but also its place in the overall operation, a new company brochure or advertisement, a news article; the choice of format should be up to each child.

Comparisons of students' work are a logical extension. Were children left with the same impressions? Did they come away with the same information?

EXTENSION:

A thank-you letter to the host at the site is, of course, expected. This need not be a routine, mechanical task. Talk candidly with children about the problem of tone in a letter of thanks. How does one express gratitude genuinely, without falling back on what appears to be prefabricated language?

Also, tell children from the outset that each of their projects will be sent along with the letter. Recognizing that there will be a new audience for their work is likely to affect children's approaches.

NOTE: This activity can easily be adapted to small groups.

What's Really in the Comics

Many historians study popular culture: movies, song lyrics, advertising, and so on. They use popular culture as a source of information about people's values and beliefs. Children also can learn from popular culture. In this activity, the comics will be their source.

Ask children to save the comics pages of your local newspaper for several days. With

From *Writing Journals*, published by GoodYearBooks. Copyright © 1996 Linda Western.

their supplies in hand, ask them to imagine that the year is 2090 and they are archaeologists who are reviewing the comics in order to interpret what they say about the 1990s. Encourage children to be specific in their review. Which cartoons include references to current fads and speech? Which ones deal with current events? Which poke fun at human foibles? (Children may devise additional categories.) Ask them to record their findings in their archaeologists' logs.

Based on their research, ask children to draft a paragraph(s) in their logs in which they answer the question, "What do the comics tell us about the world we live in?" Encourage children to bring in examples of comic strips to support their log entries. (See McGowan, 1989, 128, for further elaboration on this activity.)

EXTENSION:

Concoct a forum for presentation of the children's results, such as a convention of the American Association of Archaeology, in 2090. Print up a program for the convention, listing children's names, their positions, and the titles of their presentations. Invite others to be convention guests: students from another class, parents, staff from your local newspapers, or others if appropriate.

A Unique Summary: Creating a Political Cartoon

Not all journal and log entries need to be written. Children can create drawings, charts, diagrams, or whatever it takes to record what they are learning and thinking about. Graphic entries may complement written remarks or even substitute for them. In this activity, children summarize their study on a particular historical or current event (or character) and their opinions about it by creating a cartoon.

Begin by showing children a sampling of political cartoons from your local paper. (If you need additional sources, you'll find that each Sunday's edition of *The New York Times* includes several of these cartoons from papers around the country.) Help children see that cartoonists bring their own perspectives to bear in summarizing an event and/or telling about a person's actions. They should notice that the cartoons are never neutral reports. Like editorials, they express a definite point of view.

Encourage children to use their logs as they make their own cartoon drafts. Help them organize the task by suggesting the kinds of questions they will have to answer for themselves:

> *What event or person will be the focus?*
>
> *What point am I trying to make?*
>
> *What should be said and who should say it?*
>
> *Will more than one panel be needed?*

Remind children to show their drafts to others and to make revisions based on the suggestions they hear. Provide time for sharing the final results.

EXTENSION:

Post the final versions of the cartoons on a wall outside your classroom so that others in the school can enjoy them.

NOTE: This activity can be done individually at any time during the school year, depending on what captures each child's attention.

Tying It All Together: Making a Geographic Web

In geography units, children often study particular regions. But information about regions can seem daunting and dull. How might children make decisions about such information? How might they organize it in ways that make sense to them? Creating a geography web as an ongoing project is one approach.

Ask children to reserve a double-page spread in their learning logs for a web similar to the one below (Figure 14). Each of the major regions your class will be studying—deserts, mountains, plains, the tropics, for example—should be represented as one of the web's major branches. Then, as children read about these areas and watch videos and films that are included in your study, ask them to use what they have learned to create the body of the web, perhaps adding subheads as well as details. They should also keep an ongoing list of where they got their information. Over time, both the webs and the lists should grow to provide an effective summary of what children have learned from many sources.

From *Writing Journals*, published by GoodYearBooks. Copyright © 1996 Linda Western.

A Geographic Web

Figure 14

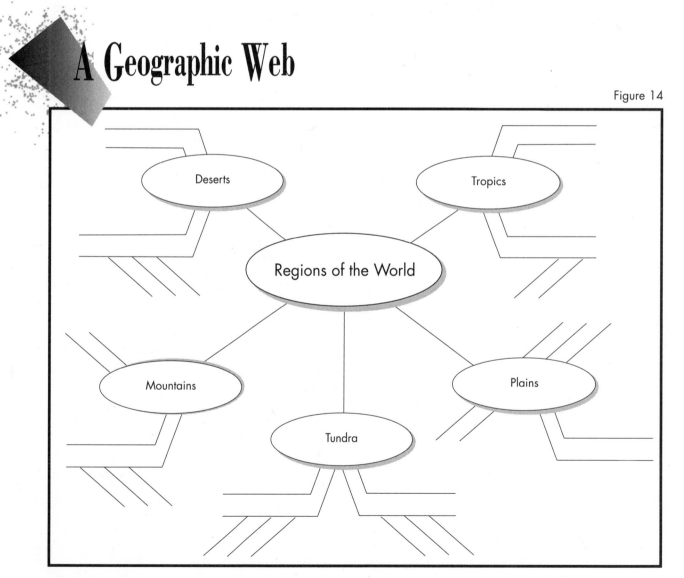

Deserts

Tropics

Regions of the World

Mountains

Plains

Tundra

In small groups, children can combine their individual webs into one large web. (This can be created on the chalkboard or on large sheets of butcher paper.) Together, children can settle on the headings they wish to use, compare data, and enter in the information they decide upon. Their finished webs should also list the sources of information children used to gather the information. Information thus organized in webs can serve as the basis for essays and stories.

What Music Can Tell Us About History

Folk songs provide us with a window on the world of the people who first sang them. Folk lyrics tell us about every facet of life; the tones and rhythms of the music tell something about the climate of the times.

This learning log activity engages children in discovering what folk songs can teach us about American history. Begin by playing some recordings of folk songs or looking together at those that are  included in the song books used by your school's music classes. Ask children to listen carefully and/or read through the lyrics, and note in their logs what stories they tell: about places, a particular time period, problems, people, work being done, etc. Have children consider, too, what we learn from the music. (This need not involve technical analysis. Children can simply tell whether tunes sound jaunty, earnest, mournful.) Talk together about the discoveries and observations.

Now children are ready to launch their own search of resources in your school and local libraries. Again, ask them to consider the same questions: What stories do the lyrics tell? What can we learn from the sounds of the music? (If they cannot read music, encourage children to find someone to sing the songs to them.)

Then, ask children to compare what they have learned from the folk songs with what they have learned in other sources. What was work like on the barges that hauled freight? They are likely to get insights from "The Erie Canal." What happened to those caught up in the dust storms of the 1930s? Children will get an inside look through the lyrics of "So Long, It's Been Good to Know You," which Woody Guthrie wrote to commemorate the experience he and half a million other people faced. There are many other fascinating examples. When their research is complete, ask children to present their findings to the class in words and in song!

NOTE: Most libraries have collections of folk songs that could be used here, but three recently published books are particularly helpful:

Axelrod, A., commentator. (1991). *Songs of the Wild West.* New York: The Metropolitan Museum of Art and Simon & Schuster.

In this volume, 45 songs sung by the cowboys and settlers of the Old West are paired with works of art, which portray the westward expansion, from the collections of The Metropolitan Museum of Art, New York, and the Buffalo Bill Historical Center, Cody, Wyoming. Explanatory notes are included for every song.

Cohn, A., compiler. (1993). *From Sea to Shining Sea, A Treasury of American Folklore and Folk Songs.* New York: Scholastic, Inc.

This collection of 140 American folk tales, folk songs, poems, and essays is organized according to historical contexts. Over 300 original illustrations were created for this volume by leading children's book artists. Brief explanatory notes also are included.

Krull, K., collector and arranger. (1992). *Gonna Sing My Head Off! American Folk Songs for Children.* (A. Garns, Illus.) New York: Alfred A. Knopf.

The table of contents indicates where each of the 62 songs in this book originates. Every song is illustrated and accompanied by an introductory note.

EXTENSION:

The scope of this activity can be widened to a study of folk songs from other countries. Children can examine library resources—books, records, tapes and disks—and talk with relatives and neighbors who may have songs to share that originated outside the U.S. Again, children's logs will serve as a handy repository for the information they gather.

Developing an Inquiry Chart (I-Chart)

James Hoffman (1992) proposes a particularly interesting strategy that can easily be adapted for use with children's learning logs in social studies units. It is called the Inquiry Chart (I-Chart).

Hoffman uses the subject of Christopher Columbus to show how the I-Chart can work. In his example, children identify three or four main questions to be answered in their study of Columbus. This process could easily be adapted to other topics. For example, in studying the pilgrims, questions could include: Why did they leave for America? What happened during their journey? What problems did they face when they arrived? How did they solve them? Children can enter these questions as headers across the horizontal axis of a chart like the one on page 61 (Figure 15). This chart can be re-created on a two-page spread.

The first horizontal row is labeled **What We Know.** Here, each child writes in whatever s/he already knows or believes in response to the questions above. Each of the next three horizontal rows is devoted to what can be learned from a particular resource. (Hoffman uses two books of nonfiction and an encyclopedia article about Columbus, but movies, videos, even the class textbook could be used.) In the last horizontal row, children summarize the information in each vertical column. Note that additional columns can be added. Hoffman heads one as **Other Interesting Facts & Figures** and another, **New Questions.** Days, even weeks, may be needed to complete the chart as children pursue their research.

Inquiry Chart

Figure 15

An inquiry chart about_____

Topic	Question 1	Question 2	Question 3	Question 4	Other Facts	New Questions
What We Know						
Source #1						
Source #2						
Source #3						
SUMMARY						

Then in pairs or small groups, children can compare their completed charts. What sources did they use? Were they able to answer their questions? Are any questions left unanswered? Did their research cause them to change their minds about anything they wrote in the **What We Know** column? They may want to combine their charts and make a much larger one, either on the chalkboard or on a large piece of butcher paper.

Children can put their I-Chart entries to work as they take their study farther. Entries can serve as the basis for developing a report to the class, creating a story, drawing a map, writing a play—the list of possibilities is a long one.

You can also help children to use their entries in making evaluations of their sources. Based on their entries, which sources were most helpful in answering questions? Which one raised the most questions? Which contributed the most interesting additional facts? Ask children to evaluate the usefulness of the I-Chart, too. Was organizing information in this way helpful? Do they wish to use the chart again?

NOTE: See Hoffman's article for an elaboration on this strategy and additional activity suggestions. (See page 136 for this reference.)

Reader Response Journals

OBSERVATIONS AND INTERACTIONS

Understanding Consequences

Adults know it is important to weigh consequences and make informed choices. But children do not develop these skills easily. This journal activity seeks to help children think about consequences by viewing them through the eyes of a character in a story.

Select a work of historical fiction in which the main character must make an important choice(s). Tell the class that it is a story about choices. As you read the story to them, they should try to notice the problems of choice that arise. Stop reading at pivotal points in the plot and ask children to describe not only the choices the character faces, but also what the consequences of each choice would be. For example, in Jean Craighead George's *Julie of the Wolves* (1974), should Julie turn back to the tundra or join her father? What would the advantages or benefits of each choice be, in Julie's eyes? What would the costs or dis-advantages be, again, as Julie would see them? Based on these considerations, what would Julie's best choice be?

Children can create a chart in their journals like the one on page 63 (Figure 16) in order to organize their responses. Once complete, these charts can be made into transparencies or recopied on the chalkboard so that students can discuss their ideas, compare them with those of others, and finally compare them with what does happen in the story.

From *Writing Journals*, published by GoodYearBooks. Copyright © 1996 Linda Western.

The Consequences of Choice

Figure 16

_____'s problem is: _____

In trying to solve the problem, s/he has the following choices:

SOLUTION 1 (description)

Advantages/Benefits:	Disadvantages/Costs:

SOLUTION 2 (description)

Advantages/Benefits:	Disadvantages/Costs:

SOLUTION 3 (description)

Advantages/Benefits:	Disadvantages/Costs:

The solution providing the best combination of costs and benefits is _____ because:

Illustrations Tell a Story, Too

Children's entries here can be used in many ways. For example, entries in the "best choice" section of the charts might be recast to form a new final chapter for the story.

And, from exercises of this sort it is a short step to exercises with computer software designed to simulate real world situations—past and present—which enable children to take on the role of a decision-maker whose choices have important consequences. For example, with Oregon Trail, by MECC, children choose a role they wish to take (banker, farmer, carpenter), what supplies to pack or their trek along the Oregon Trail, the pace at which they will travel, and so on. Children see that each choice along the way directly affects what happens to them later in the journey. Oregon Trail is just one of a number of such programs.

Book illustrations often teach us a great deal about settings, both historical and contemporary. Through a book's pictures, we can learn about the geographical characteristics of an area as well as how its people live, dress, travel, work, etc.

Children can make these discoveries for themselves, using their reader response journals to record their findings. Ask them to make a grid like the one below (Figure 17). Each vertical column should indicate which illustration is being studied; the horizontal rows should be named according to aspects of the area and life being studied: food, clothing, food, transportation, work being done, etc. Then, as they read, children can fill in the chart. Their completed grids will provide an interesting supplement to class study and discussion.

There are many picture books to choose from. Some appeal to a wide range of audiences. For example, primary and middle-grade children can use Arnold Lobel's *On the Day Peter Stuyvesant Sailed into Town* (1971) to envision

Figure 17

	Page ____	Page ____	Page ____	Page ____	Page ____
clothing					
transportation					
food					
work					

what New Amsterdam looked like in 1647, at least as Lobel saw it. For views of the Southwest, children can explore books by Byrd Baylor, (illustrated by Peter Parnall), such as, *Hawk, I'm Your Brother* (1976). The cultural heritage and art of Native American peoples is depicted well in stories and illustrations that refer to specific nations, such as *The Girl Who Loved Wild Horses* (1982), by Paul Goble. Readers of all ages gain insights from books like Muriel and Tom Feelings' *Jambo Means Hello: A Swahili Alphabet Book* (1974).

Some picture books are best suited for children beyond the primary grades. *Nettie's Trip South* (1987), by Ann Turner (illustrated by Ronald Himler), for example, provides readers with important insights into the horrors of the slave trade in Virginia shortly before the Civil War; *Watch the Stars Come Out* (1985), by Riki Levinson (illustrated by Diane Goode), offers us views of immigrant life in the late 1890s and early 1900s.

From *Writing Journals*, published by GoodYearBooks. Copyright © 1996 Linda Western.

Facts in Fiction

Readers can often learn a great deal from fiction. Stories frequently give us insights into cultures, times, and places that are different from those we are familiar with. Children's reader response journals can be very useful in uncovering the "facts in fiction."

Save this journal activity for the close of a unit. Bring in a selection of stories related in some way to your study (such as colonial America, Europe in World War II, stories set in a particular region of the country) and ask each child to select one. As they read, ask children to use their journals to note new facts or insights they are learning about that time and/or place—insights they didn't get from their textbooks or from other sources they used during the unit. By the time children have completed their readings, their literature response journals are likely to provide them with evidence not only of what they have learned, but also of how successful an author has been in providing readers with a clear sense of time and place.

EXTENSION:

Help children find gaps in the story they're reading—places in the plot where something is not made entirely clear to the reader. It could be the look on a character's face, or gesture, or something more dramatic. Then, with this gap in mind, children can try their hand at creating a new illustration to clarify the scene. Remind them that the grids they have completed in their journals will be a source of ideas for informative background details. Later, as children present their illustrations to the class, ask them to describe how they have interpreted the character's life and times.

EXTENSION:

Ask children to tell each other informally about the books they have read, using the journal entries as the basis for their comments. Encourage children to make comparisons. Which stories seem to be the most interesting? Which raised new questions?

The comparisons can be extended. Many children may want to read a story recommended by someone else. Afterward, the two readers can talk together, comparing notes about the characters and the action as well as the setting.

Biography and History—
An Important Partnership

"Biography has provided a natural literature link to social studies for decades...
Biographies enable readers to experience real life vicariously by tapping the experiences of achievers while providing a historical context for understanding such people's lives"
(Farris and Cooper, 1994, 105).

This journal activity is designed to help children clarify the link between historical figures and the times in which they lived.

Ask everyone to choose a biography or autobiography about a historical figure of special interest to them. Before they begin reading, ask children to divide a page from their journals into four boxes. In the first box, have them write down everything they think they know about the subject of their biography. In the second, ask them to note whatever they can about the times and/or places that that person lived. Then, as they read, ask children to fill in the other two boxes. In one, they should note new information their reading reveals about the person; new data about the times and/or place should be placed in the fourth.

Show children that their entries enable them to speculate. Based on what they have read and written, does it seem that the time and place set the stage for the person's accomplishments? Or, did the person contribute to shaping his/her times? Were the person's talents uniquely well-suited to a particular set of events or could they have been applied in any number of times and places?

Of course, children can also use their journal entries to compare what they knew before they began to read with what they learned. Their entries also will allow them to make evaluations and assessments. Based on what they wrote, did they learn new material? Did their opinion of the person change? How much did they learn about the events surrounding the subject of the biography? Were questions left unanswered? Help children discover that they can use their entries as the basis of a much more interesting book talk or book report than merely reciting a chronology of the person's life.

EXTENSION:

Children can use these entries as they read another books about the same figure. A third column could be added in which they note what else they are learning. Comparing their notes on the first and second books will be helpful to children, not only in understanding more about the subject, but also in evaluating the two biographies. Which provided the most information? Which was more interesting to read?

From *Writing Journals*, published by GoodYearBooks. Copyright © 1996 Linda Western.

EXPLORATION AND RESEARCH

Little Things Mean a Lot: Studying Folk Tale Variants

We can learn a great deal about a culture through its folk tales. The values of a people are often embodied in the actions of folk tale heroes and heroines; insights into the time and setting are often seen through the challenges the characters face and the rewards they receive.

In this activity, children compare variations of a folk tale. Unlike the activity, **Once Upon A Time: A Familiar Story Pattern**, pages 23–26, which focuses on discovering commonalities in folk tales, here the emphasis is on discovering what the tales tell us about the cultures that gave birth to them.

To begin answering this question, children can create a chart like the one shown on page 68 (Figure 18) and fill it in as they read variants of a given tale. Once their charts are complete, ask children to present what they have discovered to the class, using examples from the texts and illustrations.

NOTE: The comparison in Figure 18 is based on:

Chase, R., collector. (1943). "Jack and the Bean Tree." In *The Jack Tales* (B. Williams, Jr., Illus.) 31–39. Boston: Houghton Mifflin.

Howe, J., reteller. (1989). *Jack and the Beanstalk.* Boston: Little, Brown and Company.

Titles of other folk tale variants are listed on page 79.

Children can write a modern-day version of a tale they have just looked at in several variations. Before they write, talk together about the characteristics a modern-day hero or heroine might have, what tests s/he would be put to, and how s/he would be rewarded.

Exploring Cultures through Their Tales—Tricksters Around the World

"Although tales take many forms and are told in many different languages, one striking feature is the persistence of common themes in widely dispersed and apparently unrelated cultures" (McDermott, *Adventures in Folklore: Trickster Tales*, 1989, 4).

McDermott could certainly point to tricksters as examples. Trickster tales are told by cultures around the world, and they have strong appeal for children. Some tricksters are wise and lovable while others are vengeful; some best the more powerful, while others are outwitted despite their own cleverness. Recognizing the commonalities in these tales as well as their differences can add an important and enjoyable dimension to multicultural studies.

In this activity, children study trickster tales—comparing them and making conjectures about the tales' connections to the cultures where they originated. A chart like the one on page 69 (Figure 19) can help children organize their comparisons; it can easily be copied into their journals.

After they have read or heard several trickster tales, ask children to look over their charts and make some comparisons. How are the stories alike? Are certain behaviors rewarded again and again? How are they different? Do the stories reflect the cultures where they were first told? For example, are the characters portrayed as animals

Variations of a Folk Tale

Figure 18

A comparison of *Jack and the Beanstalk,* an English tale, and *Jack and the Bean Tree,* first told in Appalachia.

	Jack and the Beanstalk	Jack and the Bean Tree	Alike	Different
MAIN CHARACTERS:	Jack: brave, foolish Mother: angry Giant's wife: helpful Giant: evil	Jack: brave, puny Mother: angry Giant's maid: helpful Giant: evil	Brave Jack Evil giant One parent Helpful person at the Giant's place	Jack begins as foolish in one and spoiled in the other
SETTING:	"Once upon a time" Cottage Giant's house	"When Jack was a real teensy boy" Jack's house in the "hills and hollers" Giant's house	Both giants' houses are at the top of a beanstalk	We don't know where the cottage is in *Jack and the Beanstalk*
PROBLEM:	Jack and his mother are poor; Jack encounters the giant	Jack encounters the giant	Each Jack sets off on his own and matches wits with the giant	Jack is poor in one version and curious in the other
REWARD:	Gold, hen, and harp	Gun, knife, and blanket	Three rewards in each story	Rewards are different

Is there anything that tells us specifically about the culture from which the tale arises?

> Yes, *Jack and the Bean Tree* is told in a regional dialect. A gun, knife, and blanket would be much more useful to a pioneer than a harp. The illustrations of this story show a farm setting while those in *Jack and the Beanstalk* don't show a specific place.

From *Writing Journals,* published by GoodYearBooks. Copyright © 1996 Linda Western.

Figure 19

Origin of Story	What Sort of Trickster Is S/he?	What Sort of Behavior Is Rewarded?	What Sort of Behavior Is Punished?

that could be found in the region where the tale originated? Is the climate or geography of an area reflected in the story?

Children's comparisons and conjectures should be the basis for a class presentation as they show others the stories they have read and comment about them. You may want to consider developing a class chart, like the one in children's journals, that could grow as children read other stories of this sort.

NOTE: A partial list of trickster tales children would enjoy can be found on pages 78–79.

EXTENSION:

Now that children are familiar with trickster tales, ask them to write one of their own with a contemporary setting.

 ## Discovering the World of Mythology

"Mythology—wondrous tales of gods and mortals told by people of all times and traditions…have guided generations, served as models for living life, helped individuals find their place in society. In their infinite variety, they constitute a treasure house of timeless tales" (McDermott, *The World of Mythology: Gods and Heroes*, 1989, 4).

Comparing myths from different cultures about the same general subject is a fascinating approach for children to take in studying mythology. There are many choices you and your class can make, but here let's consider myths about the seasons.

Begin with an introductory activity. In discussion, talk together about what seasons mean, both literally and figuratively. Help children to notice how the seasons of the year are rich with imagery. Throughout the ages, composers, artists, and writers have used the seasons as symbols. We rejoice with spring, a time of rebirth and regeneration. Summer has come to represent growth and harmony. Fall brings with it an awareness of aging, a loss of innocence, and a sense of impending loss. And winter is a time of sadness, loneliness, and defeat—a frozen, barren time.

Once children understand the general idea of this imagery, set them to the task of finding examples of it at work. Children's books, both stories and illustrations, will provide many. So will popular and classical music, advertisements, movies, etc. Ask children to note their discoveries in their journals.

After several days, talk together about what children have found. Then, with these "real world" experiences as background, move on to the myths themselves. The Greek myth of Demeter and Persephone (see Kris Waldherr's *Persephone and the Pomegranate: A Myth from Greece,* 1993) was later retold by the Romans with Ceres and Proserpina as the central characters (see Gerald McDermott's *Daughter of Earth, A Roman Myth,* 1984). Children can compare both these stories with the Canadian Indian tale, "How the Summer Queen Came to Canada" (in Phelps, 1981) and a slightly different telling of a tale from the northeast woodlands in "How Glooskap Found the Summer" (in Haviland, 1979). How did people centuries ago view the seasons? Are there similarities with the imagery children just discovered? Are there similarities between the myths themselves?

Ask children to review their notes on how images of the seasons are incorporated into music and writing. Encourage them to use these entries as prompts in creating their own poems, songs, stories, or even their own version of a myth about the seasons.

Looking at Biographies and Autobiographies with a Critic's Eye

There is general agreement that biographies and autobiographies can be useful resources in learning more about history. But books of this sort are not uniformly worthwhile. This journal activity helps children develop skills to judge the quality of biographies and autobiographies for themselves.

Before beginning this activity, give children some evaluative tools. Read examples of reviews of these kinds of books that appear in sources such as *Horn Book* and *School Library Journal.* What do adult reviewers look for in biographies? What do they think are important qualities?

You may also want to help children recognize the difference between biographies and autobiographies that include fictional elements such as dialogue and those that include only facts. Reading them the foreword in Jean Fritz's *Homesick: My Own Story,* (1982), might be helpful in learning to recognize the difference. For example, here she speaks about why she has mixed fact with fiction (unnumbered foreword):

> *"Since my childhood feels like a story, I decided to tell it that way, letting the events fall as they would into the shape of a story, lacing them together with fictional bits, adding a piece here and there when memory didn't give me all I needed."*

After this background, ask children to respond to questions like those on page 71 (Figure 20) in their journals as they evaluate a biography or autobiography they have read. Then, ask them to use their entries as the basis for writing a review in a way that is similar to those that were read to them at the outset of the activity. (Have sample copies of reviews available for children to look at as they write.) Include children's final reviews in a class reference file.

Evaluating Biographies

Figure 20

Subject of biography _____

Book title_____

Author _____ Date read _____

How much of the subject's life is covered?

Is the focus on the person as a person, or on his/her accomplishments?

How much does the reader learn about the time and place where the subject lived?

Does the reader learn what else was (is) happening in the world during the subject's life? Examples include:

Is dialogue included? Is it reasonable to believe that the people involved actually said those things? Why or why not?

Is there reason to believe that the book includes other fictional elements? Explain.

Is information included about the author and the research s/he might have done in preparation for writing?

I recommend (don't recommend) this biography because:

Ask children to speculate how the biography (auto-biography) would have been different if fictional elements had been added (or, alternatively, if they had been deleted). They may choose to write one segment of the biography in the alternate style.

OBSERVATIONS AND INTERACTIONS

What's Happening? A Personal Outlook on a Current Event

Ask children to select an event that is receiving ongoing attention in the media, such as the plight of the homeless, unrest in Eastern Europe or Africa, a local strike, the aftermath of a natural disaster such as an earthquake or hurricane, or the anticipation and then playing of a much publicized competition such as the Olympics. Have children follow the event through television and radio news and in the newspapers over several days (they should clip out the articles for future reference). As they do, ask children to imagine themselves as someone living through the experiences being reported. Have them use their writers' notebooks to jot down what their reactions and impressions would be.

Then, using their notes, ask children to create diary entries about the event and their imagined places in it. As they go through the drafting and editing processes, remind children to use their own voice—their writing should be true to their own personalities and likely reactions. The diaries together with the clippings should be made available for others to read.

EXTENSION:

Children could record their diary entries on tape, prefacing each entry with a date that corresponds to one of the articles. All of the articles should be organized in a booklet or folder in such a way that listeners can easily follow them as they hear the tape.

From *Writing Journals*, published by GoodYearBooks. Copyright © 1996 Linda Western.

A Fresh Look at Familiar Places: Looking at Your State (Community) as a Tourist

Tourism is big business in many places in the United States. Yet we often think of tourism as only being important someplace else; it's easy to overlook the attractions that our own communities and states have to offer. The purpose of this activity is to help children take a second look at "their own backyards," and to practice writing in a new voice: the voice of the promoter.

Begin by bringing in brochures you've gathered from a travel agent. Put them out so that children can examine them carefully; talk together about the words, pictures, and overall layouts. Then announce the new project: children, working in production teams, will create a new travel brochure for your state, area, or community. As a first step, ask everyone to use his/her writer's notebook to jot down all the things about the designated area that people might find interesting. Children can get ideas by examining local newspapers and magazines, by following local television news broadcasts, and by making their own direct observations. They also might interview their parents and other adults. Encourage children to take many perspectives as they make their entries. They should think about special buildings (state capitols, museums, educational institutions), and also aspects of the environment (lakes, rivers, parks, wildflowers, trees, animals). But they should also think about what adds interest to life in the area (fairs, parades, sporting events, concerts, and so on). In making their lists, they should think, too, about what is important to their area from a point of view other than their own. For example, while they may not

want to go to a country fair or a rock concert, others might.

With their lists in hand, ask children to talk together about what they have written. The purpose of this talk is to decide how to organize the listed items into groups and how to elaborate on the listed items. The review might disclose a need for more information in some areas.

Next, create production teams. The task of each team is to prepare a travel brochure for the area in focus. The completed brochures should be displayed for others in the school.

EXTENSION:

Have children compare their brochures with those your state bureau of tourism has prepared. Ask someone from either a travel bureau or an advertising agency to come in to discuss what s/he thinks tourists look for when they plan a trip to a new area and how the brochures prepared by the class would fit those criteria.

Learning Through Personal History

Family and local history is recognized by many social studies teachers as having an important place in the curriculum. This activity provides children with a structural outline for preparing their own personal history.

It begins with Cynthia Rylant's *When I Was Young in the Mountains* (Dutton, 1985), a picture book with appeal for readers of all ages. Present this book to children, and make it available for them to browse through on their own so that they can fully appreciate the detailed illustrations of rural Appalachian life. As they read or hear the story for a second or third time, ask children to think of what they would write if they were to create a book like Rylant's. Some children could write about another country, others about a different state or community. And some would reflect on their experiences in the same school and neighborhood.

Ask children to use their writers' notebooks over the next several days to write down their ideas of what they could include. If they wish, each separate remembrance, like Rylant's, could begin with the line, "When I was young in…" Then, using their lists, ask them to plan out what they might say on each page of a book. Show them how to develop a thumbnail sketch of each page.

Drafting and revising will come next. Finally, children will place their copy in book format and add illustrations. The finished books should be added to the classroom library.

EXTENSION:

Plan a special program for others in the school so that your class can read and show their books to an audience.

Expanding Meanings Through Poetry

Social studies instruction often involves discussion of concepts and feelings. Yet the meanings of words central to study in social studies areas (such as *choice, freedom, patriotism, segregation, immigration, prejudice*) may seem vague and remote; memorized definitions are soon forgotten. This activity is designed to help children use their own words in defining concepts.

As a class, identify together a word(s) central to your study (like *choice, democracy, immigration*). For the next few weeks ask children to play the role of word-watchers (akin to bird-watchers). As a word-watcher, each child should be on the lookout for the key word(s), using his/her notebook to record when, where, by whom, and how it was used.

Children can then draw on their entries as they write a parallel poem like the one below (Figure 21). Here the word *patriotism* is defined, but you can substitute a term appropriate for your current course of study. (The actual number of lines is up to the writer.)

Figure 21

Patriotism is _____

_____

Patriotism is _____

_____

Patriotism is _____

_____

From *Writing Journals*, published by GoodYearBooks. Copyright © 1996 Linda Western.

There are many ways to approach the actual writing process, but consider this as one possibility. After children have reviewed their word-watcher entries, set aside ten minutes of class time and ask them to use their notebooks to complete the lines. Children should write as fast as they can and write down as many ideas as they can think of. When the ten minutes are up, have them review their entries, adding some and editing others to strengthen the definition. Urge children to cross out earlier ideas that don't hold up to later review. When they are ready, ask children to draw their best definitions together and copy them into a final form that is suitable for posting on a class bulletin board.

EXTENSION:

The poems should be included in a classroom anthology, of course, but poems are best when they are read aloud. Make arrangements for another class to visit yours and assign everyone to small groups for poetry reading.

From *Writing Journals*, published by GoodYearBooks. Copyright © 1996 Linda Western.

Applying RAFT

Social studies educators endorse the use of writing activities to engage children in thoughtful exploration of social studies topics and themes. The goal of thoughtful exploration means that the writing in question must amount to more than summaries of information from textbooks or other sources. But how might teachers plan activities that go beyond summarizing? The RAFT strategy suggests several possibilities.

RAFT is an acronym for a strategy designed by Santa, Havens, and Harrison (1989) to help students focus their writing. R stands for the role of the writer—who s/he is; A stands for the audience the writing is directed to; F is for the format the writing will take; and T is for the topic itself. Children make a decision about each letter of the acronym that, in turn, shapes their report.

Writers' notebooks provide ideal places for children to implement this strategy as they develop their report plans. Let's say, for example, that the assignment is to present a report following from a study of pioneers—a typical unit of study in the middle grades.

Children have many choices in deciding on the role of the writer; they could choose to write in their own voice, through the voice of a fictional character, or in the voice of an actual historical figure.

The audience for the writing (report) can be just one other person (the recipient of a letter, for example) or the audience could be large: imagined newspaper readers, members of the legislature, radio listeners, etc.

F Format: Here again, there are many possibilities. Children can write a letter of advice, a newspaper article or editorial, a song, a poem—whichever format strikes their fancy.

T The topic should be a specific element of the unit (here, pioneers) that is of particular interest.

Based on the outlines below, imagine how the outcomes of each of these reports would differ even though they both evolved from a unit on pioneers:

> **R** — *Commander of a fort in Nebraska*
> **A** — *Leader of the wagon train*
> **F** — *Letter of advice*
> **T** — *How to succeed on the trail ahead*

or

> **R** — *One of the pioneers*
> **A** — *Herself*
> **F** — *Diary*
> **T** — *Impressions of the trip so far*

This strategy can easily be applied to much of the writing children initiate or are asked to do not only in the social studies curriculum, but in other areas of study, too.

EXTENSION:

Children could explore the consequences of their decisions by discussing how their presentation would have been different given alternate choices for R, A, F, and T.

Creating a Conversation

As children study specific periods or movements in a history or political science unit (World War II, the voyage of the Mayflower, the pioneers' journey west, the civil rights movement), ask them to imagine what two people caught up in those events might say to each other. Ask them to use their writers' notebooks to make notes on who those characters might be (they could be real or imagined) and what their dialogue might include.

Tell children that the choice of characters is theirs. They might choose well-known figures, or their dialogues might be between ordinary people: a mother saying good-bye to her soldier son before he leaves for the front, two children who spend endless days traveling across the prairie, two listeners who have just heard Dr. Martin Luther King speak.

Get children started by engaging them in role-play. Working in pairs, have them first decide on who their characters will be, what situation they are involved in, and then what they might say to each other. Encourage children to use their notebooks to jot down what conversations seem to work well and what seems stilted and unnatural. After this initial role-play, set aside time for children to write out dialogue in their notebooks. When their first drafts are complete, children can role-play again. Critiques and editing should follow until both partners in the pair are satisfied with the results. The final versions of the dialogues should be taped, with copies available in the class library for others to hear.

Your class can plan a special program in which others are invited to hear the dialogues that were created. In addition to reading the dialogues, children will have to set the stage for their audience by providing a short summary of the events that inspired the conversations.

An Eyewitness to History: Writing a Biographical Sketch

Social studies teachers use biographies as supplementary sources. Biographies elaborate the accounts of people provided in history textbooks. Biographies also highlight the intersection of the personal and the public spheres of action in history. To underscore the contributions of biography to historical understanding, consider engaging children in composing biographies.

After children have read several biographies, ask them to use their notebooks to gather information for a biographical sketch about someone they know. They may write about the experiences an older relative or neighbor has had during a particular period—World War II or the Depression, for example. Or, they may select someone who has recently emigrated. Some children may even wish to cover someone's entire lifetime. (The scope of this project should be determined by children's interests and abilities.)

Begin by working as a group to determine where information about the subject might be obtained: the subject himself/herself, photo albums, yearbooks, letters, local newspaper archives, the subject's friends, etc. Then ask children to make notebook entries drafting the questions they would like to ask the person they have

selected. Others in the class may critique the questions. Will any of them seem too personal? Will they lead to the kind of information the writer is trying to get? Children should make any necessary changes or corrections based on the responses.

Interviewing and researching will come next. Children can use their notebooks to record information as they gather it and again to organize the presentation of what they have learned. Drafting and finalizing the sketch will complete the project.

Arrange a special program and invite the subjects of the sketches to attend. Writers can read their sketches and introduce their special guests to the class.

Working as Historians Do

People who write history work initially with primary sources, such as letters, census data, institutional reports, maps, photographs, and diaries. They take information from these sources and do things with it: summarize, rearrange, synthesize, interpret. In this way they produce notes, articles, lectures, monographs, movie scripts, books, and other products. Children can learn something about this active, constructive work of the historian by taking existing information and reconstructing it into new forms for new purposes.

This activity asks children to take material written in one format and rewrite it into another. There are many possibilities. For example, children might take a newspaper report (or set of reports) on a particular current event and recreate it as a story or interview; an interview that they have read could become a play. Or, a chapter from a historical novel could be turned into an exchange of letters between the characters.

Encourage children to choose the original material and to select the new format they would most enjoy working with. Their notebooks can be used at each step along the way, from listing possible choices of the original material to planning for its transformation and writing drafts. When the transformations are completed, children should present both versions to the class.

EXTENSION:

Publish both versions, side by side, in an anthology specially created for the project. The anthology will provide an interesting addition to your classroom library.

References

A SAMPLING OF TRICKSTER TALES

Aardema, V. (1991). *Borreguita and the Coyote.* (P. Mathers, Illus.) New York: Alfred A. Knopf. [Ayutla, Mexico]

Note: *Here a lamb (borreguita) outsmarts a coyote.*

Begay, S. (1992). *Ma'ii and Cousin Horned Toad, a Traditional Navajo Story.* New York: Scholastic Inc.

Note: *Ma'ii, the coyote, is a trickster.*

Bryan, A. (1993). *Ox of the Wonderful Horns and Other African Folktales.* 2nd ed. New York: Macmillan.

Note: *Four of the stories in this collection are trickster tales.*

Cohn, A. L., compiler. (1993). *From Sea to Shining Sea.* New York: Scholastic.

Note: *See "Tricksters, on two feet, four—or more," (202-221), which includes 6 tales and 2 songs told and sung by peoples living in America.*

Ginsburg, M. (1973). *One Trick Too Many.* (H. Siegl, Illus.) New York: Dial Press. [Russian]

Note: *Though this book is out of print, it may still be available in many libraries.*

Gobel, P., reteller. (1992). *Iktomi and the Berries.* New York: Orchard Books Watts. [North American Plains Indian]

Hamilton, V. (1985). *The People Could Fly: American Black Folk Tales.* (L. Dillon and D. Dillon, Illus.) New York: Alfred A. Knopf.

Note: *See the stories of Bruh Rabbit and Doc Rabbit.*

Hastings, S., reteller. (1991). *Reynard the Fox.* (G. Percy, Illus.) New York: Morrow. [Western Europe]

Haviland, V. (1979). *North American Legends.* (A. Strugnell, Illus.) New York: Collins.

Note: *See "Raven Lets Out the Daylight" (North Pacific), and "How Coyote Stole Fire" (Plains).*

Johnston, T. (1990). *The Badger and the Magic Fan.* (T. DePaola, Illus.) New York: G. P. Putnam's Sons.

[Japan]

Lester, J. (1985). *Knee-High Man and Other Tales.* (R. Pinto, Illus.) New York: Dial Books for Young Readers. [Regional United States]

Note: See the stories of Mr. Rabbit and Mr. Bear.

Mayo, G. W. (1993). "Meet Tricky Coyote!" *Native American Trickster Tales.* New York: Walker and Company.

McDermott, G. (1982). *Anansi the Spider: A Tale From the Ashanti.* New York: Henry Holt. [Africa]

McDermott, G. (1989). "Monkey, a Trickster From the Philippines." Also, "Papagayo the Mischief-maker." *Adventures in Folklore, Trickster Tales.* New Berlin, WI: Jenson Publications.

Note: Monkey is a trickster from the Philippines; Papagayo is a trickster from South America.

McDermott, G. (1993). *Raven, a Trickster Tale From the Pacific Northwest.* New York: Harcourt Brace Jovanovich.

McDermott, G. (1990). *Tim O'Toole and the Little People.* New York: Viking. [Ireland]

McDermott, G. (1992). *Zomo the Rabbit.* New York: Harcourt Brace Jovanovich. [West Africa]

Stevens, J., reteller. (1993). *Coyote Steals the Blanket, a Ute Tale.* New York: Holiday House.

A SAMPLING OF FOLK TALE VARIANTS

CINDERELLA

Ai-Ling, L. (1990). *Yeh-Shen: A Cinderella Story From China.* (E. Young, Illus.) New York: Putnam. [Chinese]

Brown, M. (1971). *Cinderella.* New York: Macmillan. [French]

Chase, R. (1973). "Ashpet." *Grandfather Tales.* Boston: Houghton Mifflin. [Regional America]

Climo, S. (1989). *The Egyptian Cinderella.* (R. Heller, Illus.) New York: HarperCollins.

Climo, S. (1993). *The Korean Cinderella.* (R. Heller, Illus.) New York: HarperCollins.

Jacobs, J. (1989). *Tattercoats.* (M. Tomes, Illus.) New York: Putnam. [English]

Martin, R. (1992). *The Rough-Face Girl.* (D. Shannon, Illus.) New York: Putnam. [Algonquin]

Sierra, J. (1992). *The Oryx Multicultural Folktale Series: Cinderella.* (J. Caroselli, Illus.). Phoenix, AZ: Oryx Press. [Contains 25 Cinderella stories from around the world.]

Vuong, L. D. (1992). "The Brocaded Slipper." *The Brocaded Slipper and Other Vietnamese Tales.* (V. Mai, Illus.) New York: HarperCollins.

THE LAD AND THE NORTH WIND

Chase, R. (1943). "Jack and the Northwest Wind." *The Jack Tales.* (B. Williams, Jr., Illus.) Boston: Houghton Mifflin Co. [Southern Appalachia]

Haviland, V. (1961). "The Lad and the North Wind." *Favorite Fairy Tales Told in Norway.* (L. Weisgard, Illus.) Boston: Little, Brown & Co. [Norwegian]

Note: Though this book is out of print, it is still found in many libraries.

Jacobs, J. (1967). "The Ass, the Table, and the Stick." *English Fairy Tales.* (J. Batten, Illus.) New York: Dover. [England]

Tashjian, V. (1971). "The Enormous Genie." *Three Apples Fell From Heaven, Armenian Tales Retold.* (N. Hogrogian, Illus.) Boston: Little, Brown & Co. [Armenian]

Note: Though this book is out of print, it is still found in many libraries.

RED RIDING HOOD

Grimm, J. & Grimm, W. (1982). *Little Red Riding Hood.* (T. S. Hyman, Illus.) New York: Holiday. [German]

Perrault, C. and Montresor, B. (1991). *Little Red Riding Hood.* New York: Doubleday. [French]

Young, E. (1989). *Lon Po Po: A Red Riding Hood Story from China.* New York: Philomel.

A SAMPLING OF MYTHS EXPLAINING THE SEASONS

Haviland, V., ed. (1979). "How Glooskap Found the Summer." retold by C. G. Leland. *North American Legends.* (A. Strugnell, Illus.) New York: Collins.

McDermott, G. (1984). *Daughter of Earth, a Roman Myth.* New York: Delacorte.

Phelps, E. (1981). "How the Summer Queen Came to Canada." *The Maid of the North, Feminist Folk Tales from Around the World.* (L. Bloom, Illus.) New York: Henry Holt and Company.

Walherr, K. (1993). *Persephone and the Pomegranate: A Myth from Greece.* New York: Dial.

OTHER CHILDREN'S BOOKS REFERRED TO IN THIS SECTION

Axelrod, A., commentator. (1991). *Songs of the Wild West.* New York: The Metropolitan Museum of Art and Simon & Schuster.

Baylor, B. (1976). *Hawk, I'm Your Brother.* (P. Parnall, Illus.) New York: Macmillan.

Cohn, A., compiler. (1993). *From Sea to Shining Sea, a Treasury of American Folklore and Folk Songs.* New York: Scholastic, Inc.

Feelings, M. (1985). *Jambo Means Hello: A Swahili Alphabet Book* (T. Feelings, Illus.) New York: Dial.

Fritz, J. (1982). *Homesick: My Own Story.* (M. Tomes, Illus.) New York: Putnam.

George, J. C. (1974). *Julie of the Wolves.* (J. Schoenherr, Illus.) New York: HarperCollins.

Goble, P. (1982). *The Girl Who Loved Wild Horses.* New York: Macmillan.

Krull, K., collector and arranger. (1992). *Gonna Sing My Head Off! American Folk Songs for Children.* (A. Garns, Illus.) New York: Alred A. Knopf.

Levinson, R. (1985). *Watch the Stars Come Out.* (D. Goode, Illus.) New York: E. P. Dutton.

Lobel, A. (1971). *On the Day Peter Stuyvesant Sailed into Town.* New York: HarperCollins.

Rylant, C. (1982). *When I Was Young in the Mountains.* (D. Goode, Illus.) New York: E. P. Dutton.

Turner, A. (1987). *Nettie's Trip South.* (R. Himler, Illus.) New York: Macmillan.

Journal Writing and Science

From *Writing Journals*, published by GoodYearBooks. Copyright © 1996 Linda Western.

An Overview

Learning Logs

OBSERVATIONS AND INTERACTIONS

What Would Happen If ...?
Making Connections: Creating a K-W-L Chart
Things Would Be Different Without ...
Science in the World Around Us
Gathering Data: An Introduction to Taking Surveys

EXPLORATION AND RESEARCH

The Observing Scientist
Making Comparisons
Categorizing Information: Creating an Attribute Chart
Conducting Interviews
RESPONSE, Learning Logs, and the Textbook
The Log, a Map, and a Textbook

Reader Response Journals

OBSERVATIONS AND INTERACTIONS

Science Fact, Science Fiction
Similes, Metaphors, and Science
Poetry and Science
Biography and Science

EXPLORATION AND RESEARCH

Science in the Kitchen
Animals as Symbols: Yesterday and Today
Explanations in Science and Explanations in Folklore
Exploring Science Magazines
Learning to Evaluate Nonfiction

Writers' Notebooks

OBSERVATIONS AND INTERACTIONS

I Wonder Why...
Writing Explanations: Directions for an Experiment
It Depends on How You Look at It: Writing for Different Purposes
Applying Information

EXPLORATION AND RESEARCH

Front Page News
Bringing Fact to Science Fiction
Our Own Environmental Action Handbook
Gee-Whiz Science
Good for What Ails You

References

Children's Books Referred to in This Section

Overview

How can children learn science and enjoy the process? They "need time for exploring, for making observations, for taking wrong turns, for testing ideas, for doing things over again…time for asking around, reading, and arguing; time for wrestling with unfamiliar and counterintuitive ideas and for coming to see the advantage in thinking in a different way" (Rutherford and Ahlgren, 1990, 193).

The very processes that Rutherford and Ahlgren identify as being at the heart of learning science are at the heart of journal writing, too. Observing, exploring, questioning, venturing into the unfamiliar, reworking ideas—these are the objectives of the journal activities that follow. Find time for these and other journal writing activities in your classroom. Teaching practice reveals the importance of integrating writing, through journals, with science instruction. Consider the following observations drawn from classroom experience (Grumbacher, 1987):

- The best problem-solvers are those who can relate theories to real-life experiences

- Writing helps children make the connections between experience and theory

- Making entries in learning logs on a regular basis encourages students to initiate their own questions

- Students will go beyond requirements when they are looking for answers to questions they have initiated

- Students need many opportunities to play with ideas, and work with a concept in different ways before moving on to new information

The activities in this section span a wide range of scientific fields, from astronomy to zoology. Most involve children in study that crosses traditional subject-matter lines, a fitting approach to today's science. As with all the suggestions throughout *Writing Journals*, adapt these activities to your curriculum and to the unique characteristics of your classroom. And, as you do, help your students see that the study of science can be exciting and invigorating. After all, "Inventing hypotheses or theories to imagine how the world works and then figuring out how they can be put to the test of reality is as creative as writing poetry, composing music, or designing skyscrapers" (Rutherford and Ahlgren, 1990, 7).

Learning Logs

OBSERVATIONS AND INTERACTIONS

◢ What Would Happen If...?

Predictions and beliefs most often grow out of children's prior experiences. And, those predictions and beliefs may turn out to be misconceptions. If teachers don't know about children's misconceptions, they cannot know what direction their teaching should take.

How important is this information to teaching success? Consider this anecdote, reported by Watson and Konicek (1990), about a fourth-grade classroom in Massachusetts. At the outset of a  unit on heat, children were asked to respond in their journals to the question, "What is heat?" Their teacher was astonished to read answers like these: "Sweaters are hot," "If you put a thermometer inside a hat, would it ever get hot! Ninety degrees maybe!", "Rugs get 'wicked hot'" (680-681).

Why might children have these beliefs? Living in the cold Massachusetts climate, they have heard sentences like "Put on your warm clothes" over and over again; some took the expression literally. If it weren't for a journal writing activity, that misperception would have lingered on. Instead, Watson and Konicek go on to report that the teacher adjusted her unit plans accordingly, and children carried out experiments over the next several days, wrapping thermometers in sweaters and hats, then sealing them inside plastic bags to keep out any chilling drafts. To the children's surprise, regardless of their preparations, the thermometers never budged past the reading on the room thermometer—sweaters and hats weren't hot after all.

Maybe children in your class think sweaters are hot, too! You can find out by asking them to make predictions and/or write definitions in their logs before your study of a new unit begins. Read their entries carefully. When you do, just like the fourth-grade teacher in our story, you may find yourself adjusting your teaching strategy in ways you could never have imagined.

There is an added importance to children's entries. Refer back to them once your study is complete so that children can compare what they have learned through reading and experimentation with what they wrote at the outset of their study. How much did they learn? Was there anything they had to "unlearn"? Were they surprised by the outcome of an experiment or were their hypotheses confirmed?

EXTENSION:

If experiments are a part of your study, ask children to make predictions in their logs about what would happen if one of the variables in the experiment were changed in some way. Use their entries as the basis for discussion. Wherever possible, conduct the new experiments in order to test the predictions.

◢ Making Connections: Creating a K-W-L Chart

A K-W-L chart, which stands for **Know, Want To Know** and **Learned** (Ogle, 1986, 1989), is very well-suited to science study. The chart is the product of a strategy designed to help children connect what they already know to a new area of study, to set purposes for the work ahead, and to organize what they have learned into a meaningful framework.

Children can use learning logs to work with K-W-L charts. To do so, they need only divide a two-page spread in their logs into three columns and label them as shown in Figure 22. In begin-

Figure 22

Know Want to Know Learned

Know column. Here, too, children should make corrections and additions to their own charts, based on class discussion. The completed charts can be helpful as children take the next step in their study: prepare a report, study for a test, or decide to find out more about unanswered questions.

EXTENSION:

Remind children that the K-W-L scheme will work equally well for individual study as they work to answer their own questions and puzzles. Point out, too, that the charts children construct not only record their progress as learners, but also, over time, will help them to track their interests in science.

ning a science unit, reserve time for children to list everything they think they know about the topic in the chart's **Know** column. Then help the children to pool the information they have written individually into a class K-W-L chart. (Children should add the information offered by others to their own charts.) When questions arise or when there are disagreements, entries should be made in the **Want to Know** column.

Repeat the process by asking children to work individually in listing what they would like to know about the new topic in their logs. Then, use their entries in developing the **Want to Know** column on the class chart. Again, ask children to enter the additional questions arising from discussion on their own charts.

During study, remind children to be on the lookout for answers to the questions recorded in the **Want to Know** column. Possible answers should be entered, as children discover them, in the **Learned** column of their logs. Remind children to make changes to the **Know** column, too, should they discover that an entry there proves to be incorrect. When study is complete, individual entries should be collected and entered in the **Learned** column in the class version of the chart, and necessary changes should be made in the

Things Would Be Different Without…

Helping children to relate what they are learning to their own experiences is important in every field of inquiry including science. This activity helps children to see that what they study in science has a direct bearing on their day-to-day lives.

Begin a new unit by asking children to use their learning logs in responding to the prompt, "My life would be different without _____ because …" Complete the prompt by choosing a topic related to your study. Examples might include light, gravity, heat, sound, electricity—all of which are topics in the science curriculum of grades four to six. Children's responses should be shared in a small group or with the class, and then organized into a graph or web. Taken together, their responses will provide clear proof of the importance of the subject that is about to be studied.

Repeating this activity at the close of a unit could lead to some interesting comparisons. Did children change their minds about anything they wrote before? Are there additions?

From *Writing Journals*, published by GoodYearBooks. Copyright © 1996 Linda Western.

Ask children to take one of the "differences" they have noted for their own lives and extend it to the community (nation, world). What would be the consequences of the absence on a broad scale? Their speculations could be presented to the class in a variety of forms: a song, a poem, a written or oral report, even a cartoon.

Science in the World Around Us

Textbooks do not always help children to see the relevance of science to their everyday lives. The following learning log activity helps children discover that scientific study is neither obscure nor remote.

Ask children to follow the national and local news on television and/or the radio each day for a week and note every report related in one way or another to a subject that would interest a scientist: space shuttle launchings, outbreaks of a disease, innovative products resulting from technological breakthroughs, explosions, weather phenomena—the lists should be long ones.

At the end of the week, ask the children to bring their logs back to class. Working in small groups, ask them to organize their lists according to categories. (Encourage them to devise their own category headings, too.) The compiled results should be presented to the class in a web or a chart. The webs and/or charts should speak for themselves—science is all around us.

Children can extend their exploration by searching through the local papers for relevant news articles. Working again in small groups, they should share their clippings and decide together on the categories they wish to use in organizing them. These findings should also be presented to the rest of the class.

Gathering Data: An Introduction to Taking Surveys

Gathering data, organizing it, and then using the results to draw conclusions are tasks central to the work of many scientists. They do so in order to answer questions, solve puzzles, and develop explanations. These are important skills for children to develop, too.

In this learning log activity, children plan and carry out a survey: they decide which data to gather, they gather it, and they use what they have learned to draw conclusions. The example below is based on looking at color preferences. (The electromagnetic spectrum is a topic that is often studied in grades four to six; color is the spectrum's visible portion.)

Begin by setting the stage for the inquiry to follow. Inform children that important decisions are often made on the basis of survey results. For example, a famous candy maker chose not to add any blue candy to a multi-colored variety pack after survey results showed most people didn't think blue food was appealing; a fast food restaurant chain chose orange and brown as a color scheme when a survey revealed that many people associated these colors with good food.

Next, introduce children to the idea of taking a class survey. Ask them to spend a few minutes using their learning logs to note their own responses to questions such as:

My favorite color for a jacket is …

My favorite color in flowers is…

If I were to buy a new outfit it would be…

If I were to buy a new car it would be…

I would like to paint my room…

I don't like food that is colored…

The questions can be as various as you and your class wish them to be. Use an overhead projector transparency to create a grid the whole class can see, and tally the responses (Figure 23).

Help children to use the tally marks on the completed grid in drawing conclusions, such as purple is the preferred color for flowers, or red cars are most students' favorites.

Once the procedure is clear, ask children to conduct their own survey on the topic you have selected. The questions should be their own, and they should select their own audiences. Ask them to use an overhead transparency in presenting their findings to their classmates.

Survey results vary depending on the population that makes up the sample. When a sample is broken down, results may change. Ask children to look at the surveys they conducted. How many of their responses came from children? How many from teenagers? How many from adults? Ask them to conduct another survey, asking the same question to people in each of these age groups. This time they must keep the responses from each age category separate. Do preferences vary with the age of people surveyed?

NOTE: See The Learning Log and the Daily Lesson, pages 53–54; The Learning Log and the Field Trip, page 54; and The Learning Log and the Textbook, pages 54–55. All of these activities can be easily adapted for work in science.

Survey Results

Figure 23

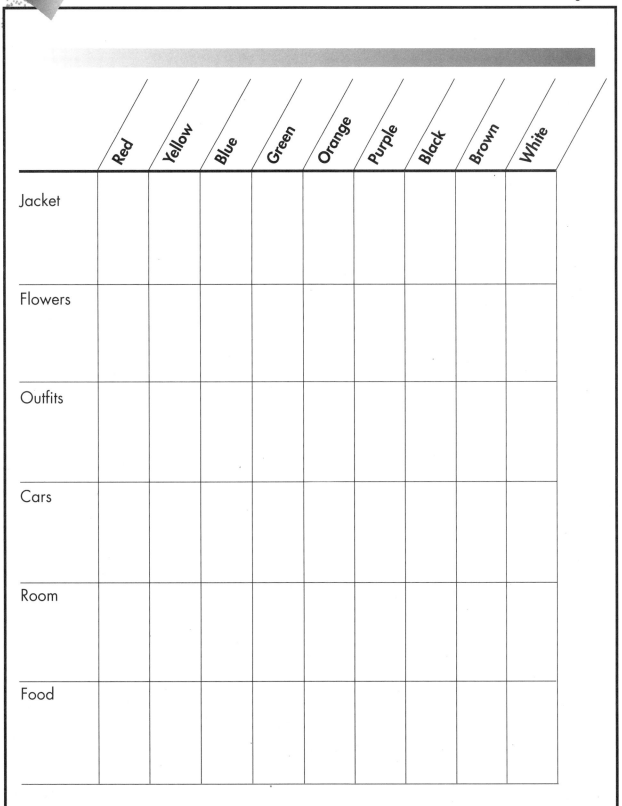

	Red	Yellow	Blue	Green	Orange	Purple	Black	Brown	White
Jacket									
Flowers									
Outfits									
Cars									
Room									
Food									

The Observing Scientist

"Sooner or later, the validity of scientific claims is settled by referring to observations of phenomena. Hence, scientists concentrate on getting accurate data" (Rutherford and Ahlgren, 1990, 5).

Children can use their logs in learning to make the careful observations that all scientists depend upon. Begin by developing a class weather log, one in which only observations, not predictions, are recorded. Children can use instruments such as a thermometer, barometer, rain gauge, and so on, to record weather conditions each day. Show them how to log in the data they have collected from these instruments and remind them to record the time of day for each observation they make.

Once they know how to record information, ask every child to develop an observational log of his/her own that s/he will keep over a period of weeks or months. Everyone will need to begin by identifying something to study; it might be the growth of a garden, the seasonal changes in a lake or river, the development of a baby brother or sister, activity in a classroom aquarium or terrarium. Each child should be free to choose his or her study.

Remind everyone to record observations, not hypotheses or predictions. From time to time, ask children to share their observations with the class. Encourage them to show their entries to others, too. Do outside readers agree that the entries represent observations rather than opinions?

When the period of observation is over, ask children to draw conclusions from what they have observed. For example, did a baby sister learn to do many more things when she was six months old compared to when she was four months old? Did the ice on a lake melt at an accelerating rate once it began to break up? Are mice more active before or after they eat?

Devise a forum for sharing the results: a class newsletter, a mock scientific conference, or a simulated educational TV program, for example.

EXTENSION:

Ask children to compare the entries at the beginning of their observation log with those they made at the end. Are their later entries more detailed? Have they grown as researchers?

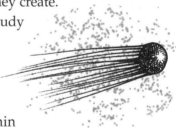

Making Comparisons

Comparing informational sources is important to the work of the scientist. Venn diagrams, like the one on page 89 (Figure 24), can help children use graphic representations to make comparisons. Learning logs are ideal places for children to keep the Venn diagrams they create.

Consider the study of outer space as an example. Children could create a Venn diagram for several specific topics within this broad study: comets, asteroids, meteoroids. Ask them to select one topic of special interest and jot down notes in their learning logs on what their textbook has to say about it. Then, have them find another source, such as a book on space in the nonfiction section of the school or local library. Again they should jot down notes in their logs on what can be learned from the second source about their selected topic.

Now it's time to fill in the Venn diagrams. Using their entries, children should use one side

From *Writing Journals*, published by GoodYearBooks. Copyright © 1996 Linda Western.

Comparing Informational Sources

Figure 24

Name _____   Date _____

Topic _____

Sources _____

_____

Information only
in Source #1   Information in
BOTH sources   Information only
in Source #2

of the diagram to show what they learned only from their textbook, the other side for what they learned only from the book they read, and in the area where the two circles overlap, they should write the information conveyed in both the textbook and the book.

EXTENSION:

The completed diagrams should provide ample material for discussion. Which source provided the most information? Were there any contradictions? How much of the information was found in both sources?

NOTE: The description of this activity suggests a comparison between a textbook and a nonfiction book. However, it can be adapted to any two sources.

Categorizing Information: Creating an Attribute Chart

Children should think of their learning logs as repositories of ideas—places to go back to again and again to retrieve information. An efficient way to store data is in an attribute chart. Setting up an organizational framework for a chart and then organizing information within it is particularly useful in science study during grades four to six.

Begin by displaying a model of an attribute chart. Show children that the headings on the horizontal axis name characteristics or attributes of the general category of things being studied. Headings on the vertical axis name specific types within that category.

Lead children in discovering how they might use an attribute chart to organize the information they are gathering. The first task in creating a chart is to decide upon which headings to use. Have children draft sample chart headings in their logs. For example, if you are studying the planets, the headings on the horizontal axis might be distance from the sun, size, and appearance; entries on the vertical axis would be the planets themselves. If you are studying nutrition, the names of vitamins and minerals might be listed across the horizontal axis, while specific foods would be listed in the vertical axis. Ask children to reproduce their drafts onto overhead transparencies so they can be shared with the class. Talk together about how the charts can be edited to offer the most usable format and reveal the most important information. Children can edit the charts in their logs accordingly and then move on to use them in recording their observations, readings, and experiments.

The example on page 91 (Figure 25) is based on a study of minerals, but a similar kind of chart can be created for many topics within your science curriculum.

EXTENSION:

Children can extend their charts or create new ones by adding to either or both of the horizontal and vertical axes.

Conducting Interviews

Many science and health units can be enriched by involving children in research with primary sources. Interviewing engages children in work of the sort that researchers in many scientific fields actually carry out. Learning logs can be central to planning the interview project.

Begin by identifying questions related to your science study that children hope to answer. Then determine who in your community could provide those answers. Depending on your unit

From *Writing Journals*, published by GoodYearBooks. Copyright © 1996 Linda Western.

Figure 25

MINERALS: Type	Hardness	Luster	Streak Color
Calcite	3	glassy	colorless
Quartz	7	glassy	colorless
Talc	1	white	non-metallic

of study, there are likely to be many sources: doctors and nurses, farmers, owners of lawn and garden centers, veterinarians, zoo directors, meteorologists, staff members of the research and development departments of local manufacturers. Decide whether you'll invite these people to visit your classroom or whether children might beable to interview them outside of school. Prior to the interview children should use their logs to jot down the interview questions they would like to ask.

In small groups, children should review their questions before the interviews. Which ones are likely to yield the most important information? Which ones aren't relevant to the study at hand? Following their review, ask children to create a master list of the questions they would like to ask. When they have completed the list, each child should record it on the left-hand side of a page in his/her learning log.

Provide time after the interview for children to use their own words in summarizing what they learned. These summaries should be entered on the right-hand column of their learning log pages. Whenever possible, the new information should be paired with the appropriate question.

Now, ask children to evaluate the information they received. Did they learn what they had hoped to? Which questions proved to be the most helpful? What questions do they wish they had asked?

EXTENSION:

Based on the information in their learning logs and their experiences with the actual interview, ask children to follow the same procedure in planning their next interview. What more do they need to find out? Who might be able to help them get answers to their questions? Should they change the interview format? Should the questions be more specific? more general? Why?

RESPONSE, Learning Logs, and the Textbook

RESPONSE is a study strategy that encourages dialogue between students and their teachers. Developed by Jeanne Jacobson (1989), this plan is designed to help children in reading and reacting to textbook assignments. It lends itself particularly well to science study and can easily be adapted to use in children's learning logs.

Ask children to use a page from their logs to create a study sheet like the one shown on page 92 (Figure 26). Then, as they read a textbook

Study **S**heet

Figure 26

Name _____   Date _____

Reading Assignment _____

IMPORTANT POINTS: As you read, use your own words to tell what information you find to be important. For each fact you write, include the page where you found it.

QUESTIONS: Write down the questions that occur to you as you read. Be sure to include page numbers. We will talk about many of these questions in class discussion. If you want an immediate answer, put an asterisk (*) by your question.

NEW WORDS/CONCEPTS/NAMES: Write down the new words, concepts, or names that you discovered while reading. Include the page numbers where you found them. Put an asterisk (*) next to anything you would like to have explained.

assignment, ask children to respond to each of the three sections: **Important Points, Questions, and New Words/Concepts/Names.** Encourage children to use their own words to summarize in a sentence or two each **Important Point.** Remind them to note the page where they found each point as well. Similarly, they should note the pages where questions arise and where new terms and concepts appear so that it will be easy to go back later and clear up possible misunderstandings.

Teachers are likely to learn a great deal as they read students' RESPONSE sheets. They can quickly see whether children are focusing on central concepts and understanding them. They can address questions and misunderstandings in subsequent lessons. They can also encourage children in their study by writing a direct response of their own ("there's so much information in this section of our book; you've done a great job of summarizing it" or "I can see why you are having trouble understanding this term; we'll talk more about it in class").

Children can use their entries using this study strategy during class discussion, and in preparation for projects and tests.

EXTENSION:

The RESPONSE strategy also lends itself to a group activity. Children can share what they have written with each other, editing and adding to their own worksheets in the process, as they work toward creating a group-made RESPONSE worksheet to share with the teacher.

The Log, a Map, and a Textbook

Science study can overwhelm some children. They complain that there is too much information to remember, too many details to keep straight. Learning logs offer places for children to sort and prioritize the facts they are studying. In doing so, there are a number of strategies they can use.

This strategy for organizing information was adapted from Hanf (1971), by Heimlich and Pittelman (1986). It can be incorporated into a learning log activity after children have studied a particular topic and have begun reviewing material in preparation for a next step: a project, report, or test.

Children begin by creating a map (or web) in their logs. The center of the map names the topic being studied. For our purposes, let's use magnets. (See page 94, Figure 27.) Children skim through the section of the textbook they have just read and copy the section's headings onto the radiating lines. Then, with their books closed, they fill in as much information as they can remember on the appropriate lines radiating from the headings.

When children have finished, ask them to work in small groups, developing a map together that incorporates the details of what each of them has written. Encourage them to make corrections and additions to their own maps during this session. Then ask children to reread the textbook assignment. Should additional information be added? corrected?

Children should find their edited maps very useful in taking the next steps in their study. They also will provide a permanent record of what children have learned.

A Scientific Web

Figure 27

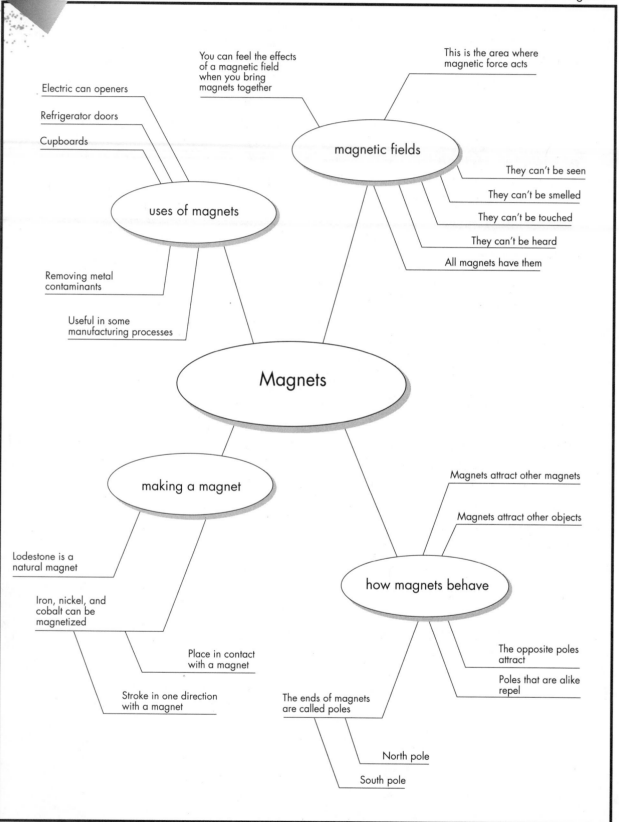

From *Writing Journals*, published by GoodYearBooks. Copyright © 1996 Linda Western.

The advantages of this kind of mapping are twofold. Children's initial maps provide them with a good understanding of what they need to learn when they compare their work with the completed group map. On the other hand, mapping is not a testing procedure; children may use the activity to learn fom one another. Help children to use their maps in evaluating their own learning progress by talking about their experiences in creating and then editing them.

Reader Response Journals

OBSERVATIONS AND INTERACTIONS

Science Fact, Science Fiction

Many science curricula in grades four to six include study related to our solar system or, more generally, to outer space. Add an extra dimension to your factual study by linking it to children's exploration of science fiction with an outer-space setting. Begin by asking children to tell about the science fiction they have read or seen in a movie or on television. How was outer space described? Did anyone live there? What special accommodations did people have to make who traveled there? How much of what they read or saw seemed to be based on fact?

Next, tell children that during the new unit on outer space, they will take another look at science fiction, this time watching for which parts of the story could actually happen and which ones are made up (fictional). In making these decisions, they will draw on the new information they are learning in science class. Children may  choose to reread a favorite story with an outer-space setting, or choose a new one. (Because science fiction typically is not easy reading, consider including the option of watching science fiction on television or at the movies for those children who can't find an appropriate book.)

Observations can be logged in children's reader response journals by dividing a journal page into four boxes. The top left box should be labeled **True** and the box at the bottom left should be labeled **False.** Then, as they read or watch, ask children to note which elements in the story they believe could be true about space life and travel and which ones could not, using the appropriate box.

After your class science study is complete, ask children to return to this journal page. In the second column, opposite each entry, ask them to comment on what they have written. Do they still believe their entries in the **True** box are scientifically accurate? What about their entries in the **False** box—do children still believe that what they have noted has no basis in fact? Encourage children to also note which of their first entries they now have questions about. These unanswered questions could launch further study.

This journal page should help children in making evaluations of the science fiction they sampled. How much of what they just read or saw was based on fact? How much was created? Was the author able to weave in enough factual information to make the story appear plausible? Why or why not?

EXTENSION:

Encourage children to explore science fiction further. Ask your librarian to help them locate choices, or look under the heading "Science Fiction" in Subject Guide to Children's Books in Print. *After a fair exposure, ask children to comment on their reactions to this genre. Is this the kind of book they would like to read more of? Why or why not?*

Similes, Metaphors, and Science

Similes and metaphors aren't reserved only for literature and poetry. All of us use these conventions in our everyday speech (see pages 29–30 for another discussion of simile and metaphor). Writers of nonfiction rely on similes and metaphors, too, as they explain new concepts by comparing them with things their readers already know about.

Nonfiction for children offers many examples. In *Storms* (1989), for instance, Seymour Simon compares a tornado to a vacuum cleaner:

"Like the hose of an enormous vacuum cleaner, the tornado picks up loose materials and whirls them aloft. In less than fifteen minutes, the funnel cloud becomes clogged with dirt and air and can no longer suck up any more" (unnumbered).

Introduce this use of metaphor to children by showing them several examples from nonfiction prose. Then set children on a search through nonfiction, written in a picture book format, for new examples. (The search could be carried out over a period of weeks, as an ongoing part of children's more general reading, in class and at home.) Ask children to record their findings in their reader response journals. Encourage them to include commentary on selected similes and metaphors. What is being compared to what? In what ways is the one thing said to resemble the other? Did the comparison lead them to a better understanding? Why or why not?

Cover a bulletin board with a large sheet of butcher paper and encourage children to write in the similes and metaphors they have discovered.

EXTENSION:

Ask children to develop a list of comparisons (similes and metaphors) that they might want to use in explaining a term, occurrence, or creature they are learning about in science class. Entries on the list can be used at any time in writing or presenting a report, creating a poem, drawing a picture, and so on.

Poetry and Science

In stories, poems, and paintings, writers and artists reveal their fascination with the natural world and its relation to human life. How do they see nature? What do they assume about its importance in human affairs? Children can explore these questions and have fun doing so by reading about nature as poets see it. Examples of nature poetry can be found in many places. Here are just a few:

Ask your librarian to gather together books of poetry that are related to the science unit your class is engaged in. Set the books out and encourage children to browse through them, using their reader response journals to note which ones add information to what they already know about a topic, which ones mirror feelings they have had about a topic (fear, wondering, amusement) and which ones help them to think about a topic in a new way. Schedule a poetry reading where children read the best of the poems they have sampled.

A Few Sources of Nature Poetry

Adoff, A. (1991). *In for Winter, Out for Spring.* (J. Pinkney, Illus.) New York: Harcourt Brace Jovanovich. Reminiscent of a journal format, this volume of poems chronicles the seasons of the year through the eyes of a family.

Fleischman, P. (1988). *Joyful Noise: Poems for Two Voices.* (E. Beddows, Illus.) New York: HarperCollins. As the title suggests, these poems need to be read aloud, either by two people or in two voices, in order to capture the rhythm and sounds that reveal so much about the insects they tell about.

Koch, K. and Farrell, K., selectors and introducers. (1985). *Talking to the Sun: An Illustrated Anthology of Poems for Young People.* New York: The Metropolitan Museum of Art and Henry Holt and Company. Several sections of this anthology are devoted to subjects that correlate with science study. Poems from many sources (including African chants, European lullabies, Japanese haiku, and American Indian verse) are sometimes accompanied by explanatory notes and always illustrated by works of art from the Museum's collection.

Lewis, J. P. (1991). *Earth Verses and Water Rhymes.* (R. Sabuda, Illus.) New York: Atheneum. Poems of snow, fog, wind, and rain are each presented on a double-page spread against a backdrop of a vivid linoleum-cut print.

Livingston, M. C. (1988). *Space Songs.* (L. E. Fisher, Illus.) New York: Holiday House. The book's dynamic paintings bring concrete poems like "Moon" and "Meteorites" to life.

Encourage children to write their own poems about something that has particularly interested them during your unit of study. Perhaps they will want to model the form of the poem they write after one they have read and particularly enjoyed.

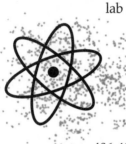

Biography and Science

Biography can pique children's interest in a topic and serve as a "bridge" to the information they will read in textbooks and other nonfictional sources. For example, the biography of an atomic scientist "...might dress the researcher in a lab coat and let the reader follow an experience step by step until the climactic moment when the scientist sees the foggy trails of atomic particles in a cloud chamber" (Glazer and Williams, 1979, 406-407). They add that a reader who is disenchanted by his/her textbook could find its material easier once s/he has experienced these "sights, sounds, and smells of the lab where the textbook knowledge originated" (407).

Ask your school librarian to gather together a number of biographies of men and women who have made contributions to the full range of scientific disciplines so that children can select the ones they wish to read from a variety of choices. Before they begin reading, ask children to divide a page from their reader response journals into two columns. They should label the first, **About the Person**, and the second, **About the Scientific Work**. Then, as they read, ask them to make notes in the appropriate columns. What does the biography tell them about what the person is (was) like? What do they learn about the scientific work s/he did?

By the time they have finished the book, their entries should enable children to make evaluations. Did most of what they read revolve around the subject or, instead, on the scientific discoveries attributed to him/her? How much information did the biographer provide? Are readers left with questions or is their curiosity satisfied?

EXTENSION:

Ask children to compare the scientific information they gathered in the biography with coverage of that topic in their textbooks. Which provides more information? Which is written in the most interesting manner? What are the strengths of the textbook? What are the strengths of the biography?

Science in the Kitchen

Nutritional content in food—or the lack thereof—has made front page news recently. But we don't have to wait for the headlines to find out what's really in the food we eat. Many recently published cookbooks include information for readers to use in interpreting and applying nutritional information. As a part of a unit on nutrition, talk about the usefulness of the material in these cookbook sections to healthy meal planning and eating. Show children an example such as *Betty Crocker's Cookbook* (1985). It includes a section on the basic food groups, defines words such as carbohydrates and proteins, and offers guidelines to help readers understand nutritional information provided through charts showing the vitamin, protein, carbohydrate, fat, and sodium content in various recipes.

After your discussion, set children on an exploration of the cookbooks at home and/or at the local library. Their task is to discover what information the cookbooks contain besides recipes. The children should use their journals to record what they find. They may want to devise a chart to organize their notes. Whatever their method, encourage them to answer questions like these:

What general information does each cookbook provide about the basic food groups?

What kinds of analyses are made of vitamin content?

Are there analyses of fat, sodium, protein, and carbohydrate content?

Do readers know how many calories are in each serving?

Do readers know how large a serving size is?

Is the information easy to read and use? Why or why not?

Based on their entries, ask children to present the cookbook they find to be the most informative to the class, explaining the reasons behind their choices.

EXTENSION:

Children can write brief annotations of the selected books. These annotations should be compiled into a "Recommended List" of cookbooks which, in turn, can be duplicated and sent home for students and their families to use.

Animals as Symbols: Yesterday and Today

Nearly every science textbook used in grades one through six includes chapters on animals, insects, and spiders. Throughout their elementary school years, children learn about these creatures' characteristics, habits and their adaptations to environments. This journal activity adds an extra dimension to that study by engaging children in discovering the special role nonhuman creatures play in folk literature.

Animals, insects, and spiders appear as characters in many folk tales, fables, and myths. The antagonists are sometimes predators and prey in the natural world (the fox and hen, for example). In some cases, a particular characteristic becomes the focus of the plot and is used to develop a theme (the industriousness of the ant is central to the well-known fable about the grasshopper and the ant). Often the character is used as a symbol for an important trait such as steadfastness and courage, duplicity, loyalty or love. See, for example, the story from the Osage, "How the Spider Symbol Came to the People," in *Keepers of the Animals, Native American Stories and Wildlife Activities for Children* (1991). The character can even come to symbolize a phenomenon in the natural world that is of great importance to the people who first told the story. For example, in *Toad Is the Uncle of Heaven: A Vietnamese Folk Tale* (1985), we read that the toad is a symbol of rain.

Ask your school librarian to help you collect a set of examples like these to share. Then set children on their own hunt through the library's folk tale section in search of stories in which animals take on important roles. Ask them to select one or two particularly interesting examples.

Now it's time to begin making use of the reader response journals. Ask children to divide a page from their journals into two columns. They should use the first to note what is learned about the animal characters through the text and illustrations in the books they have chosen. Next, ask them to seek out factual information in the library or in their textbooks about the same creatures and briefly summarize what they have learned in the second column.

Encourage children to make comparisons based on their entries. Does the factual information they have discovered in any way correspond to the characterizations and symbolic meanings the animals take on in the stories? (For example, in the Osage story, we hear the spider say, "'I am patient. I watch and I wait. Then all things come to me.' The chief saw that it was so. Thus the spider became one of the symbols of the Osage people" (Caduto and Bruchac, 31). In *Toad Is the Uncle of Heaven*, the King tells Toad to simply croak when rain is needed; the story ends, "When Uncle Toad croaks rain will soon follow" (Lee, unnumbered). Are spiders relatively inactive after their webs are spun? Do they wait for their "food supply" to come to them? Do toads really croak before a rain? What do the textbooks and other informational sources say?

Children can use their entries as they tell others in the class about the tales they have studied, sharing both fact and fiction.

EXTENSION:

Animals still have symbolic significance for modern-day peoples. Ask children to spend several days paying special attention to advertisements in newspapers, magazines, and on television. Ask them to note in their journals which animals are used in advertising (the bull in Merrill Lynch ads), as car names (Mercury Cougar, Ford Pinto), as product or service names (Greyhound bus). Encourage them to share their lists and talk together about why particular animals were selected. Is there a connection between their actual characteristics and what they are intended to symbolize?

From *Writing Journals*, published by GoodYearBooks. Copyright © 1996 Linda Western.

Explanations in Science and Explanations in Folklore

People created stories explaining natural phenomena long before they had scientific explanations. These stories have been passed down through the centuries and are part of the folklore of cultures around the world.

Today, many of these stories are retold in individual volumes as well as in anthologies. For example, the Nigerian tale, *Why the Sky Is Far Away*, retold by Mary-Joan Gerson (1992), answers the question its title poses. Gretchen Mayo's *Star Tales, North American Indian Stories About the Stars* (1987), is a collection of 15 stories first told by peoples from the plains to the seacoasts explaining the formation of the constellations. Sections of *Folk Stories of the Hmong*, collected by Norma Livo and Dia Cha (1991), are devoted to how and why stories. There are many others.

At an appropriate time during your science study (a unit on our solar system, for example), ask your librarian to gather together a selection of these tales and myths for your class to enjoy. Read several together. Then, as children read on their own, ask them to make some observations in their journals. Their entries can be in response to questions like these:

Do the stories tell us anything about the people who first told them—where they lived, what the climate was like there, what animals lived nearby?

Do the stories tell us anything about the people's needs—for food, shelter, rain, sun?

Do the stories tell us about what the people feared and/or what they appreciated?

Do the stories tell us about what characteristics were valued—strength, honesty, bravery?

How complete are the explanations?

How do these early explanations differ from the scientific explanation the children are studying?

After their reading is complete, ask the children to use their notes to prepare a book talk for a group of their classmates in which they read the story and present their answers to questions like those above.

EXTENSION:

Ask children to create their own tale or myth that offers an explanation. The phenomenon they explain can be invented, too!

Exploring Science Magazines

There are a number of periodicals with a science focus that are well-suited for use with children in grades four through six. Often these magazines sit unused on library shelves, since many children are not even aware that they exist. This journal activity provides a reason for children to seek out and explore these magazines.

First, let's look at several choices, found in many public libraries, that are particularly appropriate for children in this age group:

National Geographic World (published by the National Geographic Society, 1145 17th St. N.W., Washington, DC 20036). The focus varies—animals, pets, hobbies, etc.

Odyssey (published by Cobblestone Publishing, 7 School Street, Peterborough, NH 03458). Articles, interviews, and activities on science topics of interest to children.

Owl (published by the Young Naturalist Foundation, 500-179 John Street, Toronto, Ontario M5T 3G5, Canada). Contains articles on nature and features on technology.

Ranger Rick (published by the National Wildlife Federation, 8925 Leesburg Pike, Vienna, VA 22184). Contains articles, activities, stories, and puzzles focused on developing an appreciation for conservation.

Bring in several issues of a sampling of these and the other science magazines available to you. Then divide children into small groups. Each group will look at a specific magazine, but each child in that group will look at a different issue. Ask children to set off on an exploration in search of the kind of science-related information their issues contain. They should use their reader response journals to note their findings. What are the articles about? Is the information they contain too elementary, too complicated, or "just right"? Are the activities inviting? Is the copy readable? Are the illustrations attractive and informative?

Once their reviews are complete, ask children to talk together as a group and compare their evaluations. Ask each group to share the results of the discussion with the rest of the class. If there are conflicting evaluations, all positions should be represented in the class presentation.

EXTENSION:

Ask each group to prepare a letter to the editor of the magazine under study in which children suggest articles and features they would like to see included in subsequent issues. Once children are satisfied with the draft they have prepared and have proofed it for errors, ask a volunteer to print it, using a school computer. Mail it off and wait to see whether there will be a response.

Learning to Evaluate Nonfiction

Library shelves reserved for nonfiction are often overflowing with selections. In order for children to select the titles best suited to their science reading and research needs, they should learn how to evaluate these books for themselves.

There are two main reasons for including evaluation report forms like the one on page 103 (Figure 27) in their reader response journals. First, children will have a record of the individual titles

Evaluating Nonfiction

Figure 27

Name _____ Date _____

Title _____

Author _____ Copyright Date _____

Is information easy to find?
    Is there a table of contents?...................................... ☐ Yes ☐ No
    Is there an index?.. ☐ Yes ☐ No
    Are there chapters and section headings?..................... ☐ Yes ☐ No
    Is there a glossary? .... ☐ Yes ☐ No

Is there information about the author's credentials? .... ☐ Yes ☐ No

What about the illustrations?
    Do the illustrations explain the text?......................... ☐ Yes ☐ No
    Do the illustrations add information that isn't in the text?........ ☐ Yes ☐ No
    Are the illustrations attractive?.............................. ☐ Yes ☐ No

What about the text?
    Is information clearly written?................................ ☐ Yes ☐ No
    Does the author try to cover too much?...................... ☐ Yes ☐ No
    Does the author give enough information
        to answer my questions?.................................. ☐ Yes ☐ No
    Would I read another book by this author? .... ☐ Yes ☐ No

Is it possible that information in this book is or could
    soon be outdated?... ☐ Yes ☐ No

Based on the checklist above, I think this book is_____

_____

_____

_____

they have reviewed. But perhaps even more importantly, they will be gaining experience in applying the same evaluative standards for nonfiction used by adult reviewers.

You may want to get children started on this activity by reading a book of nonfiction together and deciding as a class how it ought to be evaluated using this form as a tool.

NOTE: This evaluation report form can easily be used for all subject areas where books of nonfiction are used.

Writers' Notebooks

OBSERVATIONS AND INTERACTION

I Wonder Why...

"Questions are the loom on which science is woven. Without questions, information, observations, predictions, and hypotheses become nothing more than a tangled ball of yarn...Yet there are few things more frustrating than having question after question go unanswered. Without strategies and resources...children finally turn away from science" (Saul, 1986, 43).

The science curriculum requirements in many school districts call for children to write reports in order to extend inquiry outside of their textbooks. One problem for children in carrying out such an assignment lies in deciding what to write about. Without a focus on a question of specific interest, children are likely to do pedestrian work. Other problems lie in deciding how to begin the research process and where to get information. With deadlines pressing on them, children often fall back on two or three encyclopedia entries for their sources.

Think of this notebook activity as a long-term project. It reminds children to note questions they find to be of particular interest as the year progresses—questions related to science that they might turn into extended study, perhaps even a science fair project. Their notebooks also can serve as a place to record ideas about how to answer their questions and list sources they discover along the way that they can go back to when it's time to prepare a report.

Ask children to reserve a section in their writers' notebooks where they will organize several pages with headings like those in Figure 29 on page 105. Explain that this section will serve as a storehouse for ideas. Then, when they decide to follow up on one of their entries, they will have a head start in planning the next steps.

Talk with children from time to time about the entries they are making in this special section of their notebooks. Look at the questions they are asking. Are they questions that can be answered? Do they reflect what the questioner really wants to know? Wendy Saul uses the question, "What makes a cardinal's feathers red?" as an example of an ill-defined question. (Saul, 36). Is the questioner asking about the chemistry that makes something red on birds, or about the evolutionary adaptation that has led to making cardinals red? As this example so clearly illustrates, deciding on the real question being asked can have a profound impact on how to begin and carry out the research to follow. When necessary, help children recast their questions. Also, talk with them about sources and procedures. Remind children that they don't have to answer questions only by looking things up.

I Wonder Why...

Figure 27

I wonder why_____

_____

_____

Sources of Information

Books:	Media: (newspaper and magazine articles, television programs, and videos)
People:	**Experiments:**

Writing Explanations: Directions for an Experiment

Science experiments should be a key feature of children's study at all grade levels. The value of participating in a science experiment can be extended in this notebook activity. Ask children to take notes on how an experiment is being carried out—one they are observing or one they are conducting themselves: the equipment that is needed, how that equipment must be set up, the sequence of the procedure, and what to look for in the results. Then, using these notes, ask them to draft a step-by-step procedure that others could use in doing the same experiment. Provide time so that classmates can review each others' drafts, making suggestions so that the directions are clear, correct, and easily read. Finalized drafts should be recopied and given to children in another class for them to follow in conducting the same experiment.

EXTENSION:

Bring in a primary-grade science book and ask children to carry out one of the experiments it includes. Then, have them follow the same plan as above— this time with younger children in mind, drafting a step-by-step procedure, reviewing each others' drafts, and finalizing the copy. Remind them that they are writing for children who are just learning to read!

When they are satisfied with their drafts, ask a primary teacher to review the directions and comment on them. Would younger students be able to read what was written? Were all the steps included?

It Depends on How You Look at It: Writing for Different Purposes

Many children's stories feature personified animals. How are they portrayed? Some of these animal characters act like people rather than animals (James Marshall's *George and Martha* [1974]); others maintain their animal characteristics even though they can speak and think (Robert Lawson's classic, *Rabbit Hill* [1944]); still others can be a blend of both human and animal attributes (Arnold Lobel's *Frog and Toad Together* [1972]).

Good nonfiction should not mix fact and fiction. Only verifiable information or reasonable hypotheses should be presented. This notebook activity provides children with practice not only in seeing these important differences in genre, but also in trying their hands at writing in the two styles.

Ask children to select a familiar animal they would like to read more about. Their next step will be to search through the picture book section of the library for stories in which that animal is the central character. Once they have found one or two suitable books, ask children to use their notebooks to comment on how the animal they have selected is portrayed: what powers of speech and thought is it given, what traits does it have? Then ask them to look at nonfiction sources for information about the same animal. Help children to notice that unlike fiction, good nonfiction provides only the facts; settings aren't created, animals are not portrayed as being able to reason or speak.

With their reading and notebook entries as background and the selected fiction and nonfiction as models, ask children to write about the

From *Writing Journals*, published by GoodYearBooks. Copyright © 1996 Linda Western.

animal they have selected in two ways. First they will create a new episode for one of the fictional stories they have selected; next, they will create a new entry for one of the nonfictional sources they have read using additional information they have gathered. (Creating additions to existing resources will help children to recognize and imitate the two distinctly different writing styles.)

Schedule an oral reading session so that children can present the books they have read and the additions they have written. Encourage discussion that focuses on the differences between personification versus factual accounts. Post children's final versions on a bulletin board titled "Animals in Fact and Fiction."

From *Writing Journals*, published by GoodYearBooks. Copyright © 1996 Linda Western.

EXTENSION:

Encourage children to illustrate what they have written. Like the writings they illustrate, these pictures should graphically show the difference between fact and fiction.

Applying Information

In many science classes, children study how animals have adapted to their environments. The webbed feet and waterproof feathers of a duck allow it to swim in the ponds that provide its food. Hawks have curved claws for capturing the small animals they eat. An armadillo's thick plates protect it from being eaten by other animals. This writing notebook activity asks children to draw information like this together and apply it in a new context.

Begin by writing out several descriptions of hypothetical animals on the chalkboard: for example, this animal has thick fur, strong hind legs and claws, large eyes, sharp teeth, and a flexible tail; this creature has keen eyesight, sharp talons, and a lightweight covering. Ask children to elaborate on one such description in their writ-

ers' notebooks. Given this set of characteristics, where would such an animal live, how big could it be, what would it eat, who would its enemies be, what would its young look like? Remind children that though the animals they create will be fictional, such creatures should be able to survive in the real natural world given the habitat and food sources that they specify. Encourage children to show drafts of what they have written to others in a small group and to make editing changes based on the responses. Then provide time for sharing and comparing.

EXTENSION:

This can become a kind of "round-robin" activity. Working in small groups, each child should first devise a description of a hypothetical animal, pass it along to another child, and then, in turn, write a response to a description prepared by someone else.

EXPLORATION AND RESEARCH

Front Page News

Learners of all ages often develop a better understanding of what they are studying when they write about it. This writer's notebook activity engages children in presenting what they have learned in a new format that is different from the textbook or nonfiction they are reading. It involves creating a newspaper front page based on information from a science unit.

Begin by looking together at the front pages of several newspapers. Notice that the articles are not all alike. Some present news, some tell a story, some may even be editorials. Also, show children examples of science reporting. (For example, the *New York Times* includes a weekly science section.)

Then propose that children create a newspaper front page that will report and reflect upon what they will learn in their next unit of science study. Have children reserve a section of their writers' notebooks to jot down ideas for possible articles. From a unit on plants, for example, children might develop a headline story on the effects of a forest fire or on the depletion of the rain forest. Another article could be written on an experiment in which researchers compared growing results after planting identical plants in different kinds of soil. Still another might be a prediction for the growing season based on long-range weather forecasts. Though the settings and people are likely to be fictional, scientific data and principles in the articles must be accurate.

At the close of the unit, ask children to share the ideas they have noted and, in small groups, plan the front page of their paper. Children can draft their articles, have others critique them, and then rework their writing until they are pleased with the results. Each group should then put its front page together. The finished products should be displayed on a school bulletin board.

| EXTENSION: |

A number of computer software programs enable children to convert their writing into a realistic-looking newspaper format. Among them are The Newsroom *(Springboard),* The Children's Writing and Publishing Center *and* The Writing Center *(Learning Company),* Publish It! *and* Publish It! Easy *(Timeworks),* PageMaker *(Aldus), and* Mac Write II, *Pro (Claris). If you have access to software of this sort, carry the project through to production.*

Bringing Fact to Science Fiction

Good science fiction most often includes some factual material such as scientific principles, or data already proven to be true (or likely to be proven true), in order to persuade readers to suspend their disbelief. This writers' notebook activity invites children to build their own science fiction around the factual content of the science they are studying.

Begin by reading a science fiction story to the class such as Madeline L'Engle's *A Wrinkle in Time* (1976), Sylvia Engdahl's *The Far Side of Evil* (1989), or Louise Lawrence's *Calling B for Butterfly* (1982). As you read, help children to think about the elements in the story that are sheer fantasy and those that could actually have happened (see the activity, **Fact or Fantasy?** on pages 19–20). Encourage them to make similar observations as you talk together about other science fiction they have read or heard.

Then introduce the children to a new writing idea: creating a science fiction story based on ideas and facts they will learn in your next science unit. The children should reserve a special page in their writers' notebooks for notes they will take as they study. What are they learning that might be the seed of an idea for a plot or suggest special capabilities for their characters? What settings could be chosen? In a unit on nutrition, could it be the introduction by aliens of foods that suddenly yield far too many or too few calories? In a unit on outer space might a budding writer envision a collision with a new solar system? In a unit on ecology, might it be a story of a time when humans become an endangered species?

Encourage children to think of as many possibilities as they can. After your study of the unit is complete, spend time sharing their ideas for plots, settings, characters and themes.

Certainly the best extension would be one where children use their most promising ideas in developing original stories. Set aside time for children to share drafts with each other. The final versions of their stories should be published in a class book. Duplicate copies so that each writer has a copy.

Our Own Environmental Action Handbook

A number of recently published books for children offer suggestions for things individuals can do to protect the environment. They include:

Bailey, D. (1992). *What We Can Do About Protecting Nature.* New York: Watts.

Earthworks Group Staff. (1991). *Kid Heroes of the Environment: Simple Things Real Kids Are Doing to Save the Earth.* Berkeley, CA: Earthworks.

Markle, S. (1991). *The Kids' Earth Handbook.* New York: Macmillan.

McQueen, K. and Fassler, D. (1991). *Let's Talk Trash: The Kids' Book About Recycling.* Burlington, VT: Waterfront Books.

Waid, M. (1993). *What You Can Do for the Environment.* New York: Chelsea House.

Bring in a selection of books like those above, share them, and then introduce the idea of creating an environmental action handbook written by the class. Set aside time so that children can browse through these books, using their notebooks to summarize the ideas they think could be applied to and implemented in their own homes, school, and neighborhoods. Ask them to be on the lookout over the next several days for additional suggestions based on what they observe.

Then ask children to share their notebook entries as they work together in small groups. Ask each group to devise a master list of suggestions they think the class handbook could include. These lists, in turn, should be shared with the class. Here, final decisions should be made about content. Writing responsibilities for each segment should be assigned to writing teams, and drafts should be shared and revised.

Recruit volunteers to enter these drafts into the computer. Once again, children can work together in editing the final draft, first in groups and then as a class. More volunteers will be needed to enter in the last round of changes.

When the handbook is complete and duplicated, organize an assembly so that your class can introduce its project and enlist the support of others in carrying out the plans.

Send the completed handbook to your city and community newspapers along with a letter that introduces the project and describes how it was created. Given the importance of the topic, the children's work may get the attention of the press.

Gee-Whiz Science

In her highly regarded *Science Fare* (1986), Wendy Saul describes gee-whiz science as "... isolated bits of information about extremes, taken out of context and designed to shake the reader" (Saul, 9-10). She explains that while this approach to science is sometimes criticized—after all, it is only an entry point to further study—children and adults find it fascinating. They delight in knowing about things that are amazing, surprising, humorous: the size of a tyrannosaur, the weight of a hummingbird's egg, the distance in miles to our sun, for example. Peculiar facts remind us of how resistant the natural world is to simplistic efforts on our part to generalize about it.

Begin by leading children in a brainstorming session in which they volunteer the "gee-whiz" science facts that impress them. Then, introduce them to the idea of creating a "Gee-Whiz Science Book" of their own. Ask them to reserve a special section of their writers' notebooks so that over the next few weeks (or months) they have a place to record the facts and theories they learn in science that seem surprising, even amazing. Their entries don't have to be related—they can cover a full range of topics. And they don't have to come from a single source. Rather, children can draw on newspapers, radio and television news, the nonfiction they read, and, of course, their science coursework.

At the end of the search period, ask children to use their entries in creating their books. The format should be their own. Perhaps they will want to introduce each page with a "Did you know…" question. Or maybe they will want to organize their entries by topic. Whatever the choice, encourage them to include illustrations. The finished books should be added to the class library until the end of the year, when the authors should take them home for their own libraries.

EXTENSION:

This project could easily be done by a small group or even the class. Individual entries could be compiled, and editing and illustrating tasks could be shared. A classroom computer would be particularly useful to a group effort. Entries could be added to files, and editing could be done on screen.

Good for What Ails You

Cures and home remedies for common ailments are passed along from generation to generation in an oral tradition of folk medicine. Is this oral tradition trustworthy? Here is an activity designed to help children compare popular views with professional expertise. The purpose is not to ridicule anybody, however; expertise sometimes confirms Grandmother's advice!

Begin by asking the children to take out their writers' notebooks and write down everything they can remember hearing from a parent or grandparent about treating various ailments: feed a cold and starve a fever, eat an apple a day, put butter on a burn, rub snow on frostbite, and so on. Then ask the children to expand their search by asking others about home remedies they have heard about or tried, such as how to remove wood ticks, cure a cold, or get rid of a headache. Children should note the responses in their notebooks, including the names of the people they talked to.

Provide time so that children can share what they have heard with each other. Together, have them determine a way to categorize these remedies by creating an organizational chart to be displayed on the overhead projector or chalkboard. Then ask a health professional into your classroom. Ask him/her to discuss which if any of these remedies may actually be effective. For any folk remedy that is not effective, or may actually be harmful, consider reasons people may have had for believing it.

Share Alvin Schwartz's Cross Your Fingers, Spit in Your Hat: Superstitions & Other Beliefs *(1990) with your class. As its title suggests, this*

From *Writing Journals*, published by

book contains a listing of superstitions that people have handed down from generation to generation. Show children that Schwartz lists his sources in an appendix, just as they are doing in their writers' notebooks.

Introduce children to the idea of using their notebook entries to create a class "Home Remedy" book, modeled after the work of Schwartz, in which they explain the remedy, possibly even weaving a story or poem around it, and develop an appendix in which they cite the actual sources. Compiling the book and preparing it for printing on a class computer would be an excellent project for volunteers.

From *Writing Journals*, published by GoodYearBooks. Copyright © 1996 Linda Western.

References

CHILDREN'S BOOKS REFERRED TO IN THIS SECTION

Adoff, A. (1991). *In for Winter, Out for Spring.* (J. Pinkney, Illus.) New York: Harcourt Brace Jovanovich.

Bailey, D. (1992). *What We Can Do About Protecting Nature.* New York: Watts.

Earthworks Group Staff. (1991). *Kid Heroes of the Environment: Simple Things Real Kids Are Doing to Save the Earth.* Berkeley, CA: Earthworks.

Engdahl, S. (1989). *The Far Side of Evil.* New York: Macmillan.

Fleischman, P. (1988). *Joyful Noise: Poems for Two Voices.* (E. Beddows, Illus.) New York: HarperCollins.

Gerson, M. J. (1992). *Why the Sky Is Far Away: A Nigerian Folktale.* (C. Golembe, Illus.) Boston: Little, Brown and Company.

Koch, K. and Farrell, K., selectors and introducers. (1985). *Talking to the Sun: An Illustrated Anthology of Poems for Young People.* New York: The Metropolitan Museum of Art and Henry Holt and Company.

Lawrence, L. (1982). *Calling B for Butterfly.* New York: HarperCollins.

Lawson, R. (1944). *Rabbit Hill.* New York: Viking.

Lee, J. M., reteller. (1985). *Toad Is the Uncle of Heaven: A Vietnamese Folk Tale.* New York: Holt, Rinehart and Winston.

L'Engle, M. (1976). *A Wrinkle in Time.* New York: Dell.

Lewis, J. P. (1991). *Earth Verses and Water Rhymes.* (R. Sabuda, Illus.) New York: Atheneum.

Livingston, M. C. (1988). *Space Songs.* (L. E. Fisher, Illus.) New York: Holiday House.

Livo, N. J. and Cha, D. (1991). *Folk Stories of the Hmong: Peoples of Laos, Thailand, and Vietnam.* Englewood, CO: Libraries Unlimited.

Lobel, A. (1972). *Frog and Toad Together.* New York: HarperCollins.

Markle, S. (1991). *The Kids' Earth Handbook.* New York: Macmillan.

Marshall, J. (1972). *George and Martha.* Boston: Houghton Mifflin.

Mayo, G. W. (1987). *Star Tales: North American Indian Stories About the Stars.* New York: Walker and Company.

McQueen, K. and Fassler, D. (1991). *Let's Talk Trash: The Kids' Book About Recycling.* Burlington, VT: Waterfront Books.

Schwartz, A. (1990). *Cross Your Fingers, Spit in Your Hat: Superstitions and Other Beliefs.* (G. Rounds, Illus.) HarperCollins, 1990.

Simon, S. (1989). *Storms.* New York: Morrow Junior Books.

Waid, M. (1993). *What You Can Do for the Environment.* New York: Chelsea House.

Journal Writing and Mathematics

An Overview

Learning Logs

OBSERVATIONS AND INTERACTIONS

Mathematics at Work

Creating Patterns

Getting to the Bottom of Things: Understanding a
  Concept

Can You Say What You See?

What Do You Think? An Exercise in Conjectures

What Did I Think Before? What Have I Learned?

EXPLORATION AND RESEARCH

Creating a Mathematics Dictionary

Where in the World Is Geometry?
   Finding and Communicating Data

Read All About It

Measuring Sense

Puzzles and Mysteries

Dollars and Sense: Taking a Closer Look at Prices

Making Connections: This Time with Science

Reader Response Journals

OBSERVATIONS AND INTERACTIONS

What's in the Fine Print?

Math at the Library: Evaluating Nonfiction

Literature in the Mathematics Class

Playing the Role of the Critic: Looking at
   Counting Books

EXPLORATION AND RESEARCH

Representing Time

Comparing Travel Times

Creating a Survey: Discovering Reader
   Preferences

Writers' Notebooks

OBSERVATIONS AND INTERACTIONS

Concrete Poetry and Mathematics

I See a Connection Between...

This Is Easy/This Is Hard

Words of Advice

EXPLORATION AND RESEARCH

Applying Understanding: Writing New Problems

A Place for Everything and Everything in Its Place:
   Practice in Categorization

Creating a Counting Book

References

Children's Books Referred to in This Section

Overview

> "A vision of an innovative mathematics program is coming alive. There is a shift in emphasis in the teaching and learning of mathematics. Teachers are encouraging children to investigate, discuss, question, and verify. They are focusing on exploration and dialogues…They are making mathematics accessible to all children."
>
> National Council of Teachers of Mathematics (1992), iv.

What is prompting this change? Many factors, but the most important is the implementation by teachers across the country of the National Council of Teachers of Mathematics' (NCTM) *Curriculum and Evaluation Standards for School Mathematics* (1989). The *Standards* are based on these assumptions (see Crosswhite, 1990):

- Mathematics instruction should emphasize knowing how rather than merely knowing that;

- Day-to-day applications of mathematics now are crucial in every corner of the working world, not merely in the special work of engineers and scientists;

- There is a sea change in the nature of and solution techniques for the problems that are now considered important.

Why? More than half of all known mathematics has been invented since World War II and computer technology has reduced the time and effort needed to carry out calculations.

What do these assumptions mean for classroom practice? A great deal:

- Mathematics instruction engages children in solving a wide range of problems.

- Children learn to use words and symbols—through prose, charts, tables, graphs, diagrams, and models—to talk and write about mathematics.

- Children reason mathematically by making conjectures, investigating possibilities, drawing conclusions, and evaluating outcomes.

- Instruction helps children to see connections between mathematics and other subjects in the curriculum, and to apply mathematics in everyday life.

Journal activities in the mathematics classroom can contribute to each of these desired outcomes. Through learning logs, reader response journals, writers' notebooks, and dialogue journals, children can practice the reasoning and communication skills that the *Standards* are designed to foster.

The following pages present several specific ideas for using journals toward this end. Some may be a perfect match with the topics you and your class are studying. Others may provide a concept and activity that you can apply in a new way. And, something in the following section may prompt entirely new journal activities, perfectly crafted by you to suit your students' interests and abilities.

In any case, a word of special encouragement is warranted before you begin. You may find that children will embrace journal writing more quickly in other subject areas than in mathematics. By the time children reach the middle grades, they tend to have definite opinions about what mathematics instruction is like—and the ideas about instruction they take for granted are just what the new standards are seeking to change! Therefore, "…a sustained effort over several weeks or… months may be needed…before they [students] come to value and expect being asked to listen, to conjecture, to reason, to model, to represent, to convince, to explain verbally and in writing, in short, to engage in rich mathematical discourse" (Lappan and Ferrini-Mundy, 1990, 488).

Learning Logs

OBSERVATIONS AND INTERACTIONS

Mathematics at Work

Children can pore over page after page of mathematics problems without ever thinking about uses of mathematics in the real world. This learning log activity will underscore the important role mathematics plays in children's daily lives.

Ask the children to carry their logs with them for a week and note how many times they use or observe any mathematical operation. For example, what mathematical operations might be involved in each of the following:

> *paying for groceries*
>
> *making change*
>
> *cooking*
>
> *reading a bus schedule*
>
> *deciding whether I have enough money to buy a candy bar*
>
> *following the score during a sporting event*
>
> *figuring out if there is enough time to do…before …*
>
> *deciding what to wear after hearing the weather forecast*

Many other day-to-day activities also could be listed. For each item, children should record some notes to explain what role mathematics plays.

After the week is up, ask children to share their notes. Are they surprised by the many things they have listed? Have they paid attention to estimating, describing, and comparing, as well as the more familiar operations? Did others mention things they overlooked?

EXTENSION:

Children can work together in small groups to categorize the things they have listed. How many are related to time? to money? to temperature? to measurement? When must they add? subtract? multiply? divide? Each group should plan to present its findings by creating a graph or table that others will find easy to understand.

Creating Patterns

Working with patterns helps children to see relationships and to observe how relationships can suggest a rule. Children can use logs to record patterns and explore their significance.

Begin this activity by presenting several patterns on the chalkboard. For example:

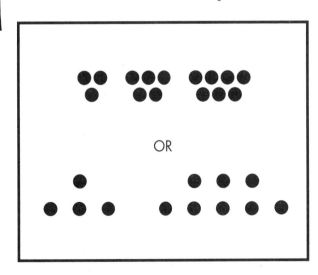

In each pattern, what comes next? What rule governs the sequence?

Ask children to draft patterns of their own in their learning logs. Remind them to ask others about the patterns they draft. Can another classmate figure out what configuration should come next? Do changes need to be made to the pattern? Can a rule be stated that explains the pattern? Once field-tested in this way, the patterns may be presented to the whole class.

EXTENSION:

Help children create a patterns bulletin board. On it they may post a sampling of their patterns and their statements of the rules that govern them.

Getting to the Bottom of Things: Understanding a Concept

While fractions provide the illustration in this activity, its underlying premise—providing children with several carefully chosen questions and/or examples, selected for their usefulness in helping children formulate generalizations—can be applied to many other topics in the mathematics curriculum.

Ask children to copy the following examples in their logs, leaving plenty of space between entries:

$$1/2 + 3/6 = 4/8$$

$$1/3 + 1/3 = 2/6$$

$$1/5 + 1/2 = 2/7$$

$$0/4 + 1/5 = 1/9$$

Over the next day or so, ask them to write about these examples. Do they agree with the answers given? What are the reasons behind their decisions?

Compile children's responses onto a handout and circulate it to the class. (Children should understand in advance that their responses will be used in this way.) Divide the class into small groups and ask children to work together in reacting to the responses. Do they agree about which equations they think are correct and which ones are not? Do they agree or disagree with the reasons others have offered? Ask the groups to summarize their discussion about each equation for the class. Use these summaries as the basis for further instruction and problem solving.

EXTENSION:

Encourage children to think of another series of examples for the rest of the class to use in an exercise of mathematical reasoning like the one above.

NOTE: See *Professional Standards for Teaching Mathematics* (1991), 90, for further elaboration of this type of activity.

Can You Say What You See?

Mathematics teachers rely heavily on chalkboard demonstrations to help students learn how to solve problems. But children don't always learn what the teacher thinks s/he is demonstrating. Here is an activity focused on that difficulty. It assumes that we learn more from demonstrations if we try to say what we see.

Encourage children to watch carefully as you take them through the steps needed to solve a particular kind of problem. After the children watch and listen to your explanations of an example or two, ask them to take out their logs and record the solution steps they are observing as you work through another example. Continue until children seem comfortable with the process. Encourage them to elaborate on their notes, adding clarification to the steps they have recorded as their understanding grows.

Then ask children to use their notes in drafting a complete, step-by-step explanation of the solution process. Will following these steps lead to a successful solution? Have children test what they have written by applying the procedure exactly as they have written it to a new problem. If the problem can't be solved by following the procedure exactly as it has been described, the children should rework their problem-solving steps.

EXTENSION:

This time ask children to first create a new problem of the sort under study and then use their solution strategy to solve it.

NOTE: This log activity can be applied throughout the school year as new problem solving skills are introduced.

What Do You Think? An Exercise in Conjectures

"Making conjectures, gathering evidence, and building an argument to support such notions are fundamental to doing mathematics. In fact, a demonstration of good reasoning should be rewarded even more than students' ability to find correct answers" (NCTM, 1989, 6).

This learning log activity calls on students to make conjectures about what a solution strategy might be. What operations will be involved? In what order should they be performed? What's the reasoning behind the strategy?

Begin by placing a new type of problem on the chalkboard. Then ask children to divide a page from their learning logs into three sections. In the first column, ask children to set out their plan, step-by-step, for arriving at an answer as well

as their reasons for thinking that the plan will work. In the second column, children should actually carry out the computations that their plans call for.

After children have had time to work through the problem, ask them to share their strategies as well as their answers. Summarize their strategies on the chalkboard and use them as the basis for further instruction, guiding children in discovering which approach to the problem is best and why.

Once instruction is complete, ask children to use the third section of their log page to note the best solution strategy that was arrived at during class discussion, as well as the logic behind it. This page can become a permanent reference for children to use as their work progresses.

EXTENSION:

This kind of activity lends itself very well to small group activities. Here, however, children, not teachers, become the instruction leaders, commenting on each others' plans, testing them, and arriving at the best solution strategy.

What Did I Think Before? What Have I Learned?

The anecdote on page 83 tells of a fourth-grade teacher's astonishment when she read her children's answers to the question, "What is heat?" Heat, children thought, is in warm clothes: "Sweaters are hot," "If you put a thermometer inside a hat, would it ever get hot! Ninety degrees maybe!"

The children's responses illustrate the important problem of misconceptions. Whatever the teacher is trying to teach, children may approach the topic with ideas that get in the way of new learning. This is so in mathematics as well as other areas of the curriculum.

Here is a learning log activity to help teachers discover what understandings (or misunderstandings) children bring to the mathematics classroom. Begin a new unit by asking children to divide a page from their learning logs into two columns. In the first, ask children to respond to a question that will lead to answers you need to know. Perhaps you will ask children to define a term. For example, "What is symmetry?" or "What is a prime number?" Or, you may ask them to respond to a question such as, "I have to use fractions when … " Read their entries carefully and plan your lessons accordingly. For example, if children think _____, you'll know that you need to contrast that view explicitly with _____ in order to get children ready for understanding _____ in a new way. Don't hesitate to tell children how much you value and rely on their entries.

After the unit of instruction is complete, go back to the prompt you began with and ask the children to respond to it in the second column. Then lead children in making comparisons. Which assumptions were borne out? Which ones proved to be incomplete or inaccurate? Compile copies of the old and new log entries onto a chart and post it prominently on a bulletin board to provide tangible proof of what the children have learned.

From *Writing Journals*, published by GoodYearBooks. Copyright © 1996 Linda Western.

EXTENSION:

Consider saving these before and after class charts throughout the year and refer to them when you begin a new unit of instruction. The charts can offer children encouragement for the learning tasks ahead by reminding them of their recent successes as learners. Taken together at the end of the year, the charts should provide an impressive record of growing mathematics mastery.

NOTE: This journal writing activity can be applied to any aspect of the mathematics curriculum in grades four to six.

Creating a Mathematics Dictionary

The name of the activity on pages 116-117 is descriptive; it involves children in trying to literally say what they see. The following activity challenges children to say what they mean when they use the language of mathematics. The ability to state something explicitly is crucial to mathematical learning.

The language of mathematics includes more than words: symbols, numbers and formulas are important as well. To help children keep a record of their skills as users of the language of mathematics, encourage them to set aside a section of their learning logs for a mathematics dictionary. Reserve time during mathematics lessons for the task of defining selected mathematics terms or symbols. Don't supply the definitions; instead, from their experiences with how the terms or symbols have been used, call upon children to formulate definitions. Many of the definitions they formulate will be written in ordinary English, but others can be stated in graphic representations (for example, a drawing that shows the relationship of a pint to a quart, or one that shows what a particular fractional amount means in relation to a real object).

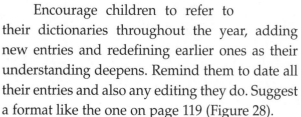

Encourage children to refer to their dictionaries throughout the year, adding new entries and redefining earlier ones as their understanding deepens. Remind them to date all their entries and also any editing they do. Suggest a format like the one on page 119 (Figure 28).

Mathematics Dictionary

Figure 28

Term or Concept	Date	Explanation

From *Writing Journals,* published by GoodYearBooks. Copyright © 1996 Linda Western.

The only order in these dictionaries is likely to be chronological, according to when a term or concept was taught during the school year. And, if the dictionaries are used to full advantage, children's entries will be marked by many additions and changes. As an extension therefore, children might create a permanent dictionary by recompiling the entries into a final draft, organizing them topically, alphabetically, or in some other way they find logical and convenient. (This would be an excellent project for desktop printing on a classroom computer.) Children can take these dictionaries home with them at the close of the school year.

Where in the World Is Geometry? Finding and Communicating Data

Children can use their learning logs to find real-world examples of the mathematical concepts and problem-solving strategies they study. Here is an example based on the geometric shapes they see every day around them in their classroom, in a room at home, at the store, and so on.

Begin by telling children that they will be going on a scavenger hunt. For what? For as many examples as they can find of particular shapes: circles, squares, rectangles, triangles, cones, hexagons, etc. On this hunt, the children will not need to gather the actual objects; rather, they can write down their findings in their logs. Add that there is something more to the assignment: once their lists are complete, children will need to organize their findings onto a table or chart; they will use these charts to summarize their data searches for others in the class.

After the children have drafted their charts, they can be copied onto an overhead transparency. Provide time for sharing.

Working in small groups or as a class, children can use the data from their own tables to create a group table. Decisions should be made about the best headings for the table and the clearest form of presentation. Then ask children to think about what they have found. Which shape seems to appear most frequently? least often? Do certain shapes appear most often in certain settings? Are there any practical reasons to explain why? Answers to these questions will suggest some interesting generalizations about geometric shapes.

Read All About It

Why do people count things? What things do people count? Is some information better suited for encoding in words than numbers? How could we find out? Here is one way.

Ask children to go the front page of a newspaper to find examples of the ways in which numbers are used; they may highlight the numbers they find or clip them out. Then ask the children to use their learning logs to decide on a scheme to organize the examples they have found. They may create categories such as these, for example, or others that are less predictable:

prices	*dates and/or times*
sports scores	*temperatures*
percents	*measurements of size*
ages	*measurements of quantity*
money	*measurements of distance*

With their charts in place, children can begin a tallying process, making a mark under the appropriate category for each time a numeric reference is made in the articles they have found. (Remind children that often they will need to make more than one tally mark for a given article.)

After the children share their results with the class, talk together about what they have found. Were they surprised in any way? What things get counted and reported numerically most often on the front page? What things don't get counted and reported numerically? Would results differ if the children studied the editorial page? the sports page? The search could be extended to include these areas.

From *Writing Journals*, published by GoodYearBooks. Copyright © 1996 Linda Western.

EXTENSION:

In order to emphasize the point that numbers and mathematical operations are useful to many people in a variety of contexts, gather together a variety of magazines from your local library that focus on particular hobbies: gardening, sailing, car mechanics, model building, cooking, decorating, outdoor sports, fitness, etc. Bring them to class and introduce them to children.

They are likely to be surprised by the range of topics and the specificity of the content. Be sure to tell children that what you have gathered is only a sampling—there are hundreds of magazines that are directed to specific interests and particular occupations, such as Design News, Popular Mechanics, Construction Equipment, *etc.*

Working in small groups, ask children to extend their search further by looking for additional examples of mathematics at work as reported in the magazines you have brought in. Provide time for discussion of their findings.

Measuring Sense

This learning log activity is designed to help children develop their sense of what measurement units are and when it is most appropriate to measure with a particular unit. Ask the children to divide a page from their logs into columns and to head each column with the name of a measurement unit (such as millimeters, centimeters or inches, meters or feet, kilometers or miles). Which units and how many you list will be for you and the class to decide.

Next, ask the children to spend five minutes using their logs to write down all the things they can think of that would most appropriately be measured by each unit. Next, provide time for children to actually carry out some measuring activities. What's the best way to measure the size of the room carpet? the distance to the gymnasium? the window pane that needs replacing?

With these experiences as background, ask children to look at their log entries again. Have they changed their minds about any entries? Encourage them to make revisions. Then, divide the class into small groups so children can share what they have written and respond to each other's questions. Why did they select a particular unit of measure? What could be measured in another way? Again, encourage children to make revisions to their logs based on their discussions.

EXTENSION:

After children have had many opportunities to apply measuring skills, ask them to create another chart (like the one described above) on a second learning log page. This time ask them to decide on new objects (distances, quantities, etc.) that could best be measured with the designated measuring units.

Working again in small groups, ask children to discuss their entries. Do the entries on the second chart demonstrate their progress in deciding upon the most appropriate measuring units?

NOTE: This activity is drawn from *Curriculum and Evaluation Standards for School Mathematics, Addenda Series, Fourth Grade Book,* **(1992), 13-14, but it can be adapted to study at any grade level.**

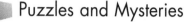 Puzzles and Mysteries

"There are so many ways to look at a problem." As adults, we all have heard statements like this one. If we've taken the words to heart, we've understood the importance of this open-minded approach to problem solving. The following learning log activity is designed to foster problem-solving flexibility.

Write a question that starts with the answer on the chalkboard: "If the answer is 24, what is the question?"

Ask children to write the answer (24) in their logs and then write down as many questions as they can think of that would fit it. For example: What is 4 x 6? 3 x 8? How many eggs in two dozen? How many inches in two feet? How much are two dimes and four pennies?

Take a large sheet of poster paper and print the answer in the middle. After sharing their questions, ask children to write them around the answer on the poster. Leave the sheet posted on a bulletin board so that more questions can be added later.

EXTENSION:

Continue to post mathematical puzzles and games on the chalkboard and encourage children to respond to them in their logs. For example, encourage children to seek out the answer to a set of clues ("I am less than 10. I am an odd number. I am more than 6. I am a prime number."). After children have had plenty of experience in solving puzzles like this one, ask them to create puzzles of their own and provide opportunities for the rest of the class to try solving them.

Dollars and Sense: Taking a Closer Look at Prices

Tying mathematics study to real-life applications is vital in developing and sustaining children's interest. This learning log activity draws on an experience that is familiar to every child in your class: paying for a purchase.

Begin by asking children if they have ever wondered who decides how much to charge for the things they buy. After a few minutes of discussion, ask children to use their learning logs to list all the questions they can think of that are related to the prices they pay. You may want to get them started by giving an example or two. Questions could include:

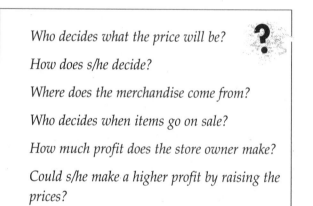

Who decides what the price will be?

How does s/he decide?

Where does the merchandise come from?

Who decides when items go on sale?

How much profit does the store owner make?

Could s/he make a higher profit by raising the prices?

Does a store owner ever lose money when items are put on sale?

Divide the class into small groups so that children can easily share the questions they have written. In turn, each group should share its questions with the class. Work together to convert these questions into a set of interview questions for a store owner or manager.

From *Writing Journals*, published by GoodYearBooks. Copyright © 1996 Linda Western.

Then, carry out the interview. Perhaps a store manager can be invited into the class to answer the children's questions. Or, perhaps children can work individually or in small groups to conduct the interviews at store sites. (In this case, letters explaining the project and requesting a time to set up an interview should be sent first.)

EXTENSION:

Answers to these questions will probably vary dramatically depending on what the products are and where they are being sold. Comparing the information gathered and making conjectures about why pricing practices and margin expectations vary from store to store, and product to product, would be a very worthwhile conclusion to this activity.

NOTE: The framework for the research project described above could be applied to many other topics under study, not only in mathematics, but across the curriculum.

Making Connections: This Time with Science

People use mathematics to study many other subjects. The applications of mathematics to science are especially important. Look for experiments that develop an understanding of both science and mathematics, and encourage children to use their logs in recording the process and the results. The experiment below is only one of many you might try.

Here the objective is to discover the germination rate of seeds. Divide the class into groups of four students. Each group will need four transparent plastic cups, masking tape, plastic wrap, paper towels, an envelope with sixty seeds, and a hand lens. Each child should get fifteen of the seeds and a cup with his/her name printed on a piece of masking tape. Then

each child should follow these steps: first, place a wet paper towel in the bottom of each cup; next, place the seeds on the towel; and then cover the cup with a sheet of wrap. Place all the cups where they can be observed but not disturbed. (The seeds should be kept moist.)

Ask the children to make a daily entry in their logs, recording their observations. When they first see growth, they should estimate how many seeds they expect to sprout, expressing that estimate as a fraction (12/15). After the seeds have sprouted, ask children to record the actual germination rate (9/15). During discussion, encourage children to compare their own estimates with the results and also to compare their results with other children's. Were germination rates similar for all students? If not, what might explain the differences?

EXTENSION:

Among the many extension possibilities, consider these: carry out the same experiment with different kinds of seeds, compare the germination rates children note with those printed on the seed packet, use the observed germination rate to estimate how many seeds would germinate if more had been planted.

NOTE: See the *NCTM Addenda Series/Grades K-6* for more suggestions of activities integrating mathematics with science. This activity was adapted from one found in the *Fourth-Grade Book*, 12.

Reader Response Journals

OBSERVATIONS AND INTERACTIONS

▶ What's in the Fine Print?

How many of us really read what's in the fine print? How "reader friendly" is that material? Maybe all of us should participate in this journal activity!

Give children copies of the back side of a billing statement from a credit card or department store charge account—the side describing the terms of the account, how interest is charged, and so on. Ask children to read the information provided and to make notes in their journals about what they have read. What can they understand? What do they have questions about? Ask them to imagine an unpaid balance and to compute the interest they think they would be charged. Their questions, comments, and computations should become the basis of a class discussion.

NOTE: Other bills can be examined, too, such as gas, electric, telephone, or water bills.

EXTENSION:

Explore the world of billing and credit by inviting a representative of a credit card company or a department store into your classroom. Before s/he arrives, ask children to work together, first in small groups and then as a class, to plan the questions they would like to ask. If needed, get them started by providing examples such as:

1) *What are the reasons for charging interest in the first place?*

2) *Who decides on what the interest rate should be? Does it ever change?*

3) *What happens when people don't pay their bills?*

4) *How does a credit card company make any money when people pay their bills on time and interest isn't added to what they owe?*

▶ Math at the Library: Evaluating Nonfiction

The children's nonfiction section of your library is likely to include a number of books on mathematics-related subjects. Many could provide materials for enrichment of mathematics lessons. This journal activity motivates children to seek these books out and look carefully inside.

Ask children to select a nonfiction book on a topic related to mathematics, for example about time, measurement, Roman numerals, estimation, or averaging. As they read, ask children to use their reader response journals in evaluating whether or not the author has presented definitions, explanations, and examples in clear and understandable ways. Suggest that they consider how they would answer questions like these in making their evaluations:

Is the vocabulary easy to understand?

Are new words defined?

Are the examples helpful?

If problems are involved, does the author show how to arrive at a solution?

Have I learned enough so that I could solve the same kind of problem on my own?

Do the illustrations help in conveying information?

Basing their comments on the entries in their journals, children can write an evaluation of the books they have chosen on file cards. The cards should be used to create a classroom "Mathematics Resources" file.

EXTENSION:

Children can plan two new pages for the book they have just reviewed. What new explanations and/or examples would they include? Ask them to present the completed pages as a part of a book talk in which they also critique what they have read.

Literature in the Mathematics Class

Mathematics is abstract. We can say that $2 + 2 = 4$ without telling what exactly we're trying to add. In fact, we don't need to have anything specific in mind; the mathematical equation means what it means without reference to anything in particular.

This abstract quality gives mathematics great power and wide scope, but it also makes mathematics seem remote, unreal, and mysterious to some people struggling to learn it. Yet students can be helped to observe quantity and quantitative relations in and among familiar things. They can learn to begin seeing things mathematically. With this purpose in mind, teachers can draw upon many sources, including children's picture books, that represent mathematical concepts concretely.

Ask children to look through the picture book section of your school or local library in search of books that they think could be used to teach a younger child something about mathematics. For example, Eric Carle's *The Very Hungry Caterpillar* (1981) or Jan Brett's *The Twelve Days of Christmas* (1986) could be helpful in teaching counting; understanding money is central to Lillian Hoban's *Arthur's Funny Money* (1981); and Carle's *The Grouchy Ladybug* (1977) offers an ideal opportunity to talk about time.

When their lists are complete, ask children to select one or more of their favorite books and bring it to class to share with others, focusing on the mathematical concept the book develops. Then, make a class list of the recommended titles. Teachers of the primary grades in your school may find the list very useful.

EXTENSION:

Help the class to draft a plan outline that could be used as the basis for teaching a younger child a mathematics concept, using one of the selected books. Show your students that devising a lesson plan involves making decisions on what to teach and how to teach it. Then, ask them to develop an actual plan based on a book of their choice. Field testing should be the next step; the children should carry out their plans, with classmates as their students. After the children make necessary revisions, they should try out their lesson plan with a young child.

Playing the Role of the Critic: Looking at Counting Books

Counting books are a staple in the picture book collections of most libraries. Ask children to find three or four of these books and compare them, making evaluative comments in their reader response journals. Responding to these questions might help children to make their evaluations:

Which book presents information most clearly?

Which book has the most attractive illustrations?

Which book is the most fun to read?

Which book is best for very young children?

Are there any that are more appropriate for older children?

Using their notes as a reference, have children present critiques of these books to others in a small group.

Representing Time

In everyday life, we like to be oriented to time and place. When we wake up in the morning, we look at the clock. If we doze off in the passenger seat of an automobile, we ask (upon waking up) where we are. The need to locate ourselves, here and now, is very basic. Clocks, mileage markers, and coordinates on maps are among the means we've devised to answer to this need.

Readers of fiction and nonfiction also seek to orient themselves to the times and places represented in the material they read. Without such an orientation, they may lose track of what they are reading. But what guides readers to a sense of time and place?

This journal activity calls for children to develop timelines based on narratives they are reading. Biographies and historical fiction are logical choices, but other narratives would work well, too. (For example, Ivy Ruckman's *Night of the Twisters* [1984] covers events spanning less than 24 hours in 130 pages.) Children can even create a timeline for narratives where actual dates and times are not explicitly noted by making inferences from the information given.

Begin by showing children an example of a timeline (your history textbook is a likely source). Point out how the scale on the timeline is like the scale on a map except that the intervals represent a designated number of years rather than miles. Tell the children that they can illustrate the passage of time in the narratives they are reading by creating timelines marking the key events.

EXTENSION:

Ask each child to select his/her favorite counting book and read it to younger children. Did these young children seem to like the book for the same reasons? Were there any differences in their responses? Provide time so that your children can reflect on the experiences of reading to others.

Children can use their journals as they read to note the key events and the times (or estimated times) associated with those events. After they have finished their books, children should review the events, crossing out those which no longer seem as important, and adding others, passed over before, that now seem significant. Help children to see that the entries on this final list will also be the entries on their timeline. Determining a scale for the timeline will be the next step. Again, their lists will be important. The quantity of time elapsing from the first entry to the last will be the determinant.

Children also can use their journals to draft their timelines, working and reworking them until they are ready for presentation to the class. Arrange the presentations in a way that will allow the children to compare the timelines they have created. Help them to notice that the sequence of events in some narratives develops over a short period of time while others extend over years; in the case of biographies, some narratives span the subject's entire life while others focus only on a specific period.

EXTENSION:

Children can create a timeline representing their own lives or the life of someone in their families. Post their work around the classroom or in school hallways.

NOTE: There is a software program called *Timeliner*, by Tom Snyder Productions, which allows children to create their own timelines on a computer. Use of this program allows children to save their work so that they can revise or add to it later. The time lines print out in a banner format. (See A Selection of Software Programs, page 138, for more information.)

Comparing Travel Times

Stories of historical fiction in which the characters travel from one place to another offer an excellent basis for children to use in determining travel times, then and now. Any number of stories could be used, but let's use the familiar *Sarah, Plain and Tall* (1985) as an example; neither the exact locations nor the specific time of the story is mentioned.

While reading, children should make notes in their journals about where the character started a journey (in our example, Maine), where s/he arrived (somewhere on the prairie), and what they guess the time frame of the story to be. They should also note any references in the story to sights characters observe along the way. Their notes will help them later in making inferences about time and place. When their reading is complete, ask children to pinpoint locations. In our example, let's say that Sarah left from Portland, Maine, and traveled to Scottsbluff, Nebraska. Then ask them to estimate a timetable (we'll say Sarah traveled in 1880).

Now it's time for children to use maps in figuring out a probable travel route for the story characters. For example, how much of the journey from Portland to Scottsbluff could Sarah have traveled by train? How much of the journey would she have to make by wagon or coach? How long would it take? Here the children will have to state some assumptions and then do some calculations. Assuming 100 miles per day by train and 30 miles per day by coach or wagon, how long would it take her to make the journey?

Using the same departure and arrival points, ask children to determine how long it would take to make the same trip today via airplane, train, bus, and/or car.

Creating a Survey: Discovering Reader Preferences

> *"Children of this age are not too young to begin thinking about the fact that how, when, and of whom we ask questions makes a difference in the results. "*
>
> *Curriculum and Evaluation Standards for School Mathematics, 3rd grade book, 23.*

We use mathematics to measure things and describe them, but each act of measuring and describing involves a prior decision, conscious or unconscious, about what to measure or describe. This activity helps children notice how decisions of this sort shape the results obtained.

Begin by asking children to talk about the books they most enjoy. Help them pool their lists and categorize the entries by type: joke books, mysteries, nonfiction, etc. Tally the responses and ask the children to draw conclusions: Most children in our class prefer _____. More boys than girls prefer _____. Then pose the questions: "Do you think reading preferences vary with age? Would children in the sixth (second, kindergarten) agree with us? How could we find out?"

To find out, the children could take a poll of other children in their school or neighborhood. Before they begin, they will need a plan: What questions will they ask in order to find out about reading preferences? How many children will they question? How many age groups will they include?

Ask each child to use his/her journal to draft a chart similar to the one on page 129 (Figure 29) to use in taking the survey. Working together in small groups, children can compare their ideas and develop a next draft. In turn, groups should present their drafts to the class in order to complete a survey form that everyone can use. Duplicate the final form so that each child has a copy.

Now it's time to take the survey. Encourage the children to talk to at least five other children, but remind them to write down each interviewee's name. If two people interview the same child, his/her responses shouldn't be counted twice!

Once the surveys are completed, children should work together in class to tabulate the results. Then, encourage children to draw conclusions based on their findings. Were enough children asked in each category? Do others need to be asked? If the sample is large enough, what do the responses reveal? For example, were joke books the choice of most second graders? Were alphabet books the least favorite of seventh graders?

Children can analyze their data further by tabulating the results according to whether the respondent was a boy or a girl. For example, do eighth grade girls like the same books as eighth grade boys?

From *Writing Journals*, published by GoodYearBooks. Copyright © 1996 Linda Western.

A Survey of Reading Preferences

Figure 29

	Kindergartners		3rd Graders		8th Graders	
	BOYS	GIRLS	BOYS	GIRLS	BOYS	GIRLS
Joke books						
Funny stories						
Mysteries						
Stories about people living today						
Stories that happened a long time ago						
Biographies						
Fairy tales						
Alphabet books						
Informational books						

Writers' Notebooks

OBSERVATIONS AND INTERACTION

Concrete Poetry and Mathematics

According to the well-known poet, Myra Cohn Livingston, "concrete poetry, often called pattern poetry or shape poetry, is a form of playing with words, ideas, letters, and art" (Livingston, 1991, 136). A section of her *Poem-Making: Ways to Begin Writing Poetry* is devoted to discussion and examples of this poetic form. Share Livingston's examples, as well as other concrete poetry with children.

While certainly concrete (shape) poems can be created in any number of ways, children could have fun creating their own using mathematical symbols—a poem about money in the shape of a dollar sign, a poem illustrating more than (or less than) written in a way that reminds readers of the comparable mathematical symbol, etc. While the initial entries in their writers' notebooks may be little more than doodling, encourage children to keep refining them until they are satisfied with the results. Children's completed concrete poems would make a fascinating bulletin board display in a school hallway.

EXTENSION:

If your classroom computer system includes the appropriate software, children might want to try their hands at creating concrete poetry on a computer.

I See a Connection Between . . .

"When mathematical ideas are also connected to everyday experiences, both in and out of school, children become aware of the usefulness of mathematics" (NCTM, 1989, 32).

Keeping the importance of making these kinds of connections in mind, consider using this writing activity with other work you do throughout the school year. As children are introduced to new mathematical concepts and problem-solving techniques, ask them to make entries in their writers' notebooks that establish links with what they already know and/or connections with possible application situations. Several journal prompts would be particularly useful in helping children make the connections:

This problem reminds me of . . .

This is what I learned before that is helping me now . . .

I can imagine that (engineers, construction workers, doctors and nurses, etc.) might have to solve problems like this when . . .

Provide ample time during mathematics class throughout the school year to share these entries. Children will certainly be able to learn from one another as they recognize connections they hadn't thought of before. You will learn from the journals, too; the information they convey about the growth of the students' understanding can help you make decisions about your instruction.

EXTENSION:

Invite people from the working world into your classroom to discuss how they apply mathematics in their jobs. Children should prepare questions they

From *Writing Journals*, published by GoodYearBooks. Copyright © 1996 Linda Western.

would like to ask during the visit. If the children have previously responded to the third question, above, they can use their entries as the basis for interview questions.

This Is Easy/This Is Hard

Ask children to set aside a section of their writers' notebooks. Then, periodically, provide time so that they can use this section in commenting on what they are doing in mathematics class and how they feel about their progress. Ask them to talk about which kinds of problems they find difficult to solve and what it is that makes them difficult. Conversely, they also should comment when things seem easy. Encourage them to speculate about what they are learning in mathematics, too, by asking questions such as "I wonder why…?" or "What would happen if …?"

Your review of these comments will provide you with a unique window on students' understanding and the effectiveness of various teaching strategies. Use these entries as the basis for helping children to overcome learning obstacles and to capitalize on learning strengths.

EXTENSION:

Encourage children to talk about their entries with others in a small group. Groups should be ideal places to share solution strategies, commiserate, and praise successes.

Words of Advice

On the first or second day of school in the fall, tell children that in the spring you will ask them to look back over their year's work in mathematics so that they can offer advice to next year's students—the kind of advice they wish they had received. They will need to reserve the back

pages of their writers' notebooks to record entries throughout the school year for this springtime project. Questions like these might prompt their responses:

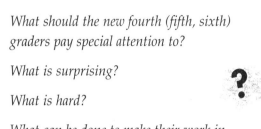

What should the new fourth (fifth, sixth) graders pay special attention to?

What is surprising?

What is hard?

What can be done to make their work in mathematics easier? more fun? How much time should they spend on homework?

Be sure to remind children to date their entries.

Sometime in May, ask the children to begin reviewing their entries. Do the things that seemed to be monumental problems in October now seem easy? What still is troublesome? Review these observations together. Then, children should begin writing. Let them know that their advice can be offered in many forms: a letter, a list, a series of warnings, a poem, and so on.

EXTENSION:

Before compiling these offerings into a collection of final drafts for the classroom library, invite next year's class in for an interview. The children should ask their visitors about their expectations for the next year, and what they'd like to learn more about. The information provided in the interviews then can be considered by your students before they complete their final drafts.

Applying Understanding: Writing New Problems

Children can clarify their understanding of the mathematical concepts they are learning by applying them in new contexts. One approach to this task is to create new versions of mathematics problems like the ones they are studying. To give a new example requires at least a tacit understanding of the principles that define the previous set of examples. The children can make their initial drafts of new problems in their writers' notebooks and then ask a partner or others in a small group to try to solve them.

Were the new problems in fact like the old ones? Are the new problems too easy or too hard? Children's notebooks are the places to resolve these questions. When they have been revised, the new problems can be presented to the whole class, either in a chalkboard demonstration or by means of a worksheet.

EXTENSION:

Ask children to create versions of mathematics problems for students a year or two younger. In addition to providing enough information to make solutions possible, they will have to decide what skills the problems should be developing and what accommodations need to be made for vocabulary. Make arrangements so that younger children can actually try solving the new problems, with your students on hand as tutors.

A Place for Everything and Everything in Its Place: Practice with Categorization

Effective communication does not always rely on words. Graphs, tables, charts, and symbols are important, too. Here children can devise a set of categories for things in their own environments. In creating these categories, children will have to think of the properties seemingly unlike objects have in common.

Ask children to select one room—your classroom, another room in the school, a room at home—and create a chart that allows them to categorize everything that room contains  (furniture, floor coverings, window coverings, decorations, toys, etc.). Remind children that they will need enough categories to encompass everything in the rooms they have selected. Their notebooks will provide an excellent practice ground for planning the final version of the chart.

EXTENSION:

Ask the children to bring in the final versions of their charts to share with others in the class. They will need to explain how they arrived at their categorization scheme and answer classmates' questions. Help children notice that there is often a wide variety in the ways things can be sorted and/or classified.

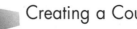

Creating a Counting Book

Begin by showing children examples of several different kinds of counting books—those that convey information, those that tell a story, and those that focus only on graphically illustrating

From *Writing Journals*, published by GoodYearBooks. Copyright © 1996 Linda Western.

what numbers mean. For example, in *Moja Means One: A Swahili Counting Book* (1976), Tom and Muriel Feelings teach readers to count to ten in Swahili, using a detailed African village scene as the backdrop for illustrating each number. Maurice Sendak's *One Was Johnny* (1962) tells the story of a boy who is beset by a growing number of obnoxious visitors—a rat and a robber, for instance—until the crowd seems overwhelming. Johnny then starts counting backwards until he is alone at last. In *Count and See* (1972), Tana Hoban uses photographs to clearly show the designated number of objects (birthday candles, eggs in a carton, and the like); there is no story line or other informational content.

After this introduction, encourage children to go to your school or local library and examine a number of counting books. They should look for those that simply illustrate the numbers, those that carry out a theme, and those that tell a story. Ask them to select one or two of their favorites to share with the class.

With their own searches and the presentations of others as background, children can begin drafting their own plans for a counting book in their notebooks. Will it have a theme? Will the text rhyme? What sorts of illustrations should be included? What age reader would enjoy the new book the most? Encourage children to share their plans with others in a small group and to use others' reactions as they develop details. Then, based on the plans, children can create their own books. (See pages 49–50 for suggestions of books that include directions for book making.)

EXTENSION:

The best of all extensions for this project is to present the new book to audiences of other children.

References

CHILDREN'S BOOKS REFERRED TO IN THIS SECTION

Brett, Jan. (1986). *The Twelve Days of Christmas.* New York: Putnam.

Carle, E. (1977). *The Grouchy Ladybug.* New York: HarperCollins.

Carle, E. (1981). *The Very Hungry Caterpillar.* New York: Putnam.

Feelings, M. (1976). *Moja Means One: A Swahili Counting Book.* New York: Dial Books.

Hoban, L. (1981). *Arthur's Funny Money.* New York: HarperCollins.

Hoban, T. (1972). *Count and See.* New York: Macmillan.

Livingston, M. C. (1991). *Poem-Making: Ways to Begin Writing Poetry.* New York: HarperCollins

MacLachlan, P. (1985). *Sarah, Plain and Tall.* New York: HarperCollins.

Ruckman, I. (1984). *Night of the Twisters.* New York: HarperCollins.

Sendak, M. (1962). *One Was Johnny: A Counting Book.* New York: HarperCollins.

Where to Learn More

References

WHAT'S SO SPECIAL ABOUT JOURNALS?

Atwell, N. (Ed.) (1990). *Coming to Know: Writing to Learn in the Intermediate Grades.* Portsmouth, NH: Heinemann.

Berthoff, A. E. (1987). "Dialectical Notebooks and the Audit of Meaning." In T. Fulwiler (Ed.), *The Journal Book* (11-18). Portsmouth, NH: Boynton/Cook Publishers.

SOME JOURNAL BASICS

Atwell, N. (1987). *In the Middle: Writing, Reading and Learning with Adolescents.* Portsmouth, NH: Boynton/Cook Publishers.

Calkins, L. M. (1991). *Living Between the Lines.* Portsmouth, NH: Heinemann.

Farris, P. J. and Cooper, S. M. (1994). *Elementary Social Studies: A Whole Language Approach.* Madison, WI: WCB Brown & Benchmark.

Fulwiler, T. (Ed.) (1987). *The Journal Book* (1-8). Portsmouth, NH: Boynton/Cook Publishers.

Moffett, J. and Wagner, B. J. (1992). *Student-Centered Language Arts, K-12, 4th Ed.* Portsmouth, NH: Boynton/Cook Publishers.

Pearson, P. D. (1993). "Teaching and Learning Reading: A Research Perspective." *Language Arts,* 70, 502-511.

Staton, J. (1987). "The Power of Responding in Dialogue Journals." In T. Fulwiler (Ed.) *The Journal Book* (47-63). Portsmouth, NH: Boynton/Cook Publishers.

GETTING STARTED

Atwell, N. (Ed.). (1990). *Coming to Know: Writing to Learn in the Intermediate Grades.* Portsmouth, NH: Heinemann.

Calkins, L. M. (1991). *Living Between the Lines.* Portsmouth, NH: Heinemann.

Moffett, J. and Wagner, B. J. (1992). *Student-Centered Language Arts, K-12, 4th Ed.* Portsmouth, NH: Boynton/Cook Publishers.

JOURNAL WRITING AND LITERATURE

Commire, A. (Ed.) (Multiple volume series). *Something About the Author: Facts and Pictures About Contemporary Authors and Illustrators of Books for Young People.* Detroit, MI: Gale Research, Inc.

Guth, D. L. (Ed.) (1976). *Letters of E. B. White.* New York: Harper and Row.

Norton, D. E. (1992). *The Impact of Literature-Based Reading.* New York: Macmillan.

Western, L. (1980). "A Comparative Study of Literature Through Folk Tale Variants." *Language Arts,* 79, 395-402.

JOURNAL WRITING AND SOCIAL STUDIES

Farris, P. J. and Cooper, S. M. (1994). *Elementary Social Studies: A Whole Language Approach.* Madison, WI: WCB Brown & Benchmark.

Hancock, M. R. (1993). "Exploring and Extending Personal Response Through Literature Response Journals." *Reading Teacher,* 46 (6), 466-474.

Hoffman, James V. (1992). "Critical Reading/Thinking Across the Curriculum: Using I-Charts to Support Learning." *Language Arts,* 69, 121-127.

Kuhrt, B. L. (1989). *The Effects of Expressive Writing on the Composing and Learning Processes of Sixth-Grade Students in Social Studies.* DeKalb, IL: Northern Illinois University.

McDermott, G. (1989). *Adventures in Folklore: Trickster Tales.* New Berlin, WI: Jenson Publications. (Now, Hilton Head Island, SC: Child Graphics Press.)

McDermott, G. (1989). *The World of Mythology: Gods and Heroes.* New Berlin, WI: Jenson Publications. (Now, Hilton Head Island, SC: Child Graphics Press.)

McGowan, T. and McGowan, M. (1989). *Telling America's Story: Teaching American History Through Children's Literature.* New Berlin, WI: Jenson Publications. (Now, Hilton Head Island, SC: Child Graphics Press.)

Moffett, J. and Wagner, B. J. (1992). *Student-Centered Language Arts, K-12, 4th Ed.* Portsmouth, NH: Boynton/Cook Publishers.

Santa, C., Havens, L. & Harrison, S. (1989). "Teaching Secondary Science Through Reading, Writing, Studying, and Problem Solving." In D. Lapp, J. Flood & N. Farnan (Eds.) *Content Area Reading and Learning.* (137-151). Englewood Cliffs, NJ: Prentice-Hall.

Walley, C. (1991). "Diaries, Logs and Journals in the Elementary Classroom." *Childhood Education,* 67 (3), 149-154.

Western, L. (1980). "A Comparative Study of Literature Through Folk Tale Variants." *Language Arts,* 57 (4), 395-402.

JOURNAL WRITING AND SCIENCE

Caduto, M. & Bruchac, J. (1991). *Keepers of the Animals: Native American Stories and Wildlife Activities for Children.* (J. K. Fadden, Illus.) Golden, CO: Fulcrum Publishing.

Glazer, J. I. & Williams III, G. (1979). *Introduction to Children's Literature.* New York: McGraw Hill.

Grumbacher, J. (1989). "How Writing Helps Physics Students Become Better Problem Solvers." In T. Fulwiler (Ed.) *The Journal Book.* (323-329). Portsmouth, NH: Boynton/Cook Publishers.

Hanf, M. B. (1971). "Mapping: A Technique for Translating Reading Into Thinking." *Journal of Reading*, 14, 225-230, 270.

Heimlich, J. E. and Pittelman, S. D. (1986). *Semantic Mapping: Classroom Applications. Newark*, DE: International Reading Association.

Jacobson, J. M. (1989). "RESPONSE: An Interactive Study Technique." *Reading Horizons*, 29 (2), 85-92.

Ogle, D. M. (1986). "K-W-L: A Teaching Model That Develops Active Reading of Expository Text." *Reading Teacher*, 39, 564-570.

Ogle, D. M. (1989). "The Know, Want To Know, Learn Strategy." In K.D. Muth (Ed.) *Children's Comprehension of Text: Research Into Practice* (205-223). Newark, DE: International Reading Association.

Rutherford, F. J. and Ahlgren, A. (1989). *Science for All Americans.* New York: Oxford University Press.

Saul, W. with Newman, A. (1986). *Science Fare, An Illustrated Guide and Catalog of Toys, Books, and Activities for Kids.* New York: HarperCollins.

Watson, B. and Konicek, R. (1990). "Teaching for Conceptual Change: Confronting Children's Experience." *Phi Delta Kappan*, May 1990, 680-685.

JOURNAL WRITING AND MATHEMATICS

Atwell, N. (1990). *Coming to Know: Writing to Learn in the Intermediate Grades.* Portsmouth, NH: Heinemann.

Crosswhite, F. J. (1990). "National Standards: A New Dimension in Professional Leadership." *School Science and Mathematics*, Volume 90 (6), 454 - 466.

Lappan, G. and Ferrini-Mundy, J. (1990). "Implementing the NCTM Curriculum and Evaluation Standards for School Mathematics in Grades 5-8: Obstacles and Opportunities." *School Science and Mathematics*, Volume 90 (6), 486 - 493.

Leiva, M. A., Series Ed. (1992). *Curriculum and Evaluation Standards for School Mathematics, Addenda Series, Grades K-6.* Reston, VA: National Council of Teachers of Mathematics.

National Council of Teachers of Mathematics. (1989). *Curriculum and Evaluation Standards for School Mathematics.* Reston, VA: NCTM.

National Council of Teachers of Mathematics. (1991). *Professional Standards for Teaching Mathematics.* Reston, VA: NCTM.

Software

From *Writing Journals*, published by GoodYearBooks. Copyright © 1996 Linda Western.

A SELECTION* OF SOFTWARE PROGRAMS APPROPRIATE FOR CHILDREN'S WRITING AND PUBLISHING IN GRADES 4-6

AppleWorks, Claris Corporation, 5201 Patrick Henry Drive, Santa Clara, CA 95052

ClarisWorks, Claris Corporation, 5201 Patrick Henry Drive, Santa Clara, CA 95052

The Children's Writing and Publishing Center, The Learning Company, 6493 Kaiser Drive, Fremont, CA 94555

MacWrite II Pro, Claris Corporation, 5201 Patrick Henry Drive, Santa Clara, CA 95052

The Newsroom, Springboard Software, Inc., 7808 Creekridge Circle, Minneapolis, MN 55435

The Oregon Trail, MECC, 3490 Lexington Ave. North, St. Paul, MN 55126

PageMaker, Aldus Corporation, 411 First Ave. So., Suite 200, Seattle, WA 98104

Publish It! and *Publish It! Easy*, Timeworks, Inc., 444 Lake Cook Road, Deerfield, IL 60015-4919

Timeliner, Tom Snyder Productions, 90 Sherman St., Cambridge, MA 02140

Writing Center, The Learning Company, 6493 Kaiser Drive, Fremont, CA 94555.

*Due to rapidly changing technology, this list should not be considered comprehensive.